# SUICIDE

## *of the*

# FITTEST

HOW THE FRISBEE / MILK DUD CONSPIRACY
IS DESTROYING WESTERN CIVILIZATION

IT IS WHAT IT IS ——

ISBN: 0985598700
ISBN-13: 9780985598709

*Do not answer a fool according to his folly.....*
*Answer a fool according to his folly.*

(Proverbs 26:4-5)

# Preface

It had been more than a year since the rough draft for this book was finished. The file was dutifully fermenting on the hard drive, awaiting some heretofore unknown catalyst. And then I found myself on a winter layover in Coconut Grove, Florida.

It feels good to leave sub-freezing weather for a week. Simply walking around in the warmth can be its own pleasurable reward. But something is amiss. Let me explain.

This municipality, like so many others, has made a "green push." Part of this green push is the noble effort to harness power from the sun. And one of the things done here, south of Miami, is the installation and attempted use of solar-powered parking meters. The meters are amazing machines. Well-designed and well-

constructed. So one has to assume the designers and builders are good at what they do.

Evidently competence only goes so far. There are some serious, obvious problems. The first meter I saw was the one shown on the previous page. This picture was taken at noon. Notice the direction of the signpost's shadow. That shadow will raise questions in the minds of those who are scientifically curious. My own curiosity prompted an informal survey, and it was shocking, and then irritating, to find that 18 units out of a total of 20 -- 90% -- have solar panels facing North. This means they've been set up in a position guaranteeing they will never receive any of the sunlight necessary to generate electricity. (Most

readers won't understand why this won't work. Trust me; I was one of those 8th grade nerds with a telescope. If you'll meet me at noon on Grand Avenue in Coconut Grove I can easily explain the problem. Otherwise we'll have to go thru a short science course. And then you'd fall asleep and never finish this book. So just trust me for now.) It is frustrating to witness such folly. How can people be so ignorant? And how can they be so wasteful with other people's money?

One obvious objection, of course, is that Coconut Grove is an isolated example. So here's more data. The picture on the left side of the page was taken at Briarcrest High School in Cordova, Tennessee. Also at noon. The solar panel for this signal is oriented North. The two others at this location are too. That's three out of three. 100%. Again, no chance to absorb solar light.

These "no light" situations highlight a fatal flaw with man's current non-linear,[1] postmodern[2] approach to life. Western culture has arrived at a lofty and technologically advanced point in history. It has done this by developing, refining, and then relying upon algebra, geometry, calculus, astronomy, metallurgy, chemistry, hard work, and sacrifice. And while that list is exhausting, it's by no means exhaustive.

But the last half-century has witnessed a destructive shift away from that kind of academic discipline. And Hollywood, probably unwittingly, has served up some appropriate commentary. Consider the movie "The Saint" where we see Dr. Emma Russell[3] step up to the front of the class and argue for a different way to solve man's challenges:

> **Student**: *But, I read somewhere that the (cold fusion) experiment couldn't be replicated. So how do we know it works?*
>
> **Dr. Emma Russell**: *Well, we don't ---- not yet. But if you remember Einstein, he **knew** the theory of relativity to be true[4] long before he could prove it... I mean he **felt** the truth. And, uh, some of us **feel** the same way about cold fusion. Because it's there, it's in nature, the raw natural power just waiting to be harnessed. And when we ignite that cold fusion fire, I mean, just imagine! There's more energy in one cubic mile of seawater than all of the known oil reserves on Earth. You could drive your car 55 million miles on a gallon of heavy water! It would be the end of pollution! Warmth for the whole world!*

This quote summarizes what is beginning to pass for academic rigor today. And, if not already there, it's coming soon to an institute of higher learning near you. (Memo from Albert Einstein to Dr. Russell: *Feeling* is not *knowing*.)

Another way of looking at this problem: It has become fashionable to go beyond simply thinking outside the lines (which is good), to removing the lines altogether (which is very bad). Example: The focus in major university curricula is becoming overwhelmingly slanted toward things like "diversity studies." This is coming at the expense of classical education.[5] People graduating out of these systems have useless degrees and much more useless training. Many are assimilated by default into public sector and municipality careers. They have no idea which way is North or South and can't even spell "compass." These are the academic zombies who are tasked with installing a city's parking meter solar panels. And the utility futilities found at Coconut Grove and Cordova are just the latest in a long list of personally witnessed examples. The problems are there for anyone to see. Walk out the door of any hotel, or go to any public place, open your eyes, and note what is happening. There's a lot of incompetence on display, and it's begging us to consider an ominous possibility: Western Civilization is disintegrating.

Time out. Before going any further, we need definitions for *Western Civilization* and *Western Culture*:

> **Western culture**, *sometimes equated with* **Western civilization** *or* **European civilization**, *refers to cultures of European and American origin, and is used very broadly to refer to a heritage of social norms, ethical values, traditional customs, religious beliefs, political systems, and specific artifacts and technologies.*
>
> *Western culture stems from two sources: the classical Period of the Greco-Roman era and the influence of Christianity.*[6]

The main purpose of this book is to present reasoned arguments, satirical observations, and hard data supporting the idea that Western Culture is committing suicide. I will thus try to convince you that this is happening because we are allowing ourselves to be exploited through our own aspirations for goodness. Another way of looking at the premise is that Western Culture's fatal flaw is its excellence. Thus the title: **Suicide of the Fittest.**

But it may be the subtitle that commands more attention. Note to reader: If you've opened this book breathlessly anticipating proof for a "Frisbee / Milk Dud Conspiracy," you're going to be disappointed. There is no conspiracy. At least not a provable one. It may look like a conspiracy, and talk like a conspiracy, but since there's an attempt here to be bound by linear, rational constraints, the claim cannot officially be made. And after all, the bar for defining what is, and what is not, a conspiracy has been forever set impossibly high by someone held in universally reverent esteem: Hillary Rodham Clinton.[7]

So the subtitle is mostly an attempt to be cute and catchy. Must've been effective, though -- you bought the book. (And if you're looking for knee-jerk justification for not reading any further, here's your big chance.)

Conspiracy theories notwithstanding, there are identifiable negative trends in American culture. A lot of them. And in the adjoining room over here we can find the usual suspects. The concurrent appearance of the negative trends along with the suspects is..........suspicious. And it suggests there might be a coherent philosophy and unified force behind our obvious downward spiral. This decline has been driven by an *institutionalized* abandonment of almost all proven avenues for excellence and achievement. As noted above, these trends and forces cannot be attributed, unmistakably, to a conspiracy. But we can make educated guesses. This book is mostly a satirical, educated guess.

Something obvious at this point -- a frightening consideration. Americans may be pawns in a supernatural conspiracy seeking to dethrone our Maker from His rightful place as God and Creator of the universe. Most Christians believe this supernatural struggle has been going on since Lucifer was banished from God's presence. If you're atheistic or agnostic, you're invited to pretend for a while. Or maybe think in terms of allegory. Just don't miss the pragmatic point: that there's evidence of a horrifying struggle being played out before our own eyes in our own homes. Don't take my word for this. Just push that small red button in the upper right-hand corner of your TV remote.

Select almost any channel. Now watch the despicable drama unfold in 52-inch, brilliant HD color right there in your own den. (We paid $1600.00 for the LCD TV and then $70.00 per month for the cable for *this*?) What we are seeing in the Earthly arena is inarguably mankind's headlong rush through mediocrity on his way to the gutter. Granted it will have to be a faith-based conjecture, but our situation has all the earmarks of a bunch of cattle being herded along by Satan. It sure looks like we're headed for Hell.

Frisbees and Milk Duds serve as metaphors for two key factors in America's decline. Frisbees represent the alternate lifestyle sought by those who see themselves as outcast. These "outcasts" have chosen a path that keeps doubling down on their perceived alienation. Example: Here is a snow-boarder who's blocking the ski-lift lines. He's not coop-erating and he appears to be insolent. We don't have to be judgmental in his particular case because a sticker on his helmet says: "I'd rather be hated than ignored."

Milk Duds represent the childish tantrums of the immature. If you're a parent, you probably won't need any help getting your mind around the imagery. For the rest of us, just picture a five year-old squeezing a fist full of candy while screaming in the grocery check-out line. Applications? I'm ashamed to say there are way too many. I'm ashamed because it appears that my generation is responsible for almost all of the chaos. It was my generation that screamed obscenities on the Washington Mall, burned draft cards and showed callous indifference to societal stand-ards of honor and decency. Looking back over four decades, we can no longer ignore how we failed society. The protestors failed by caus-ing the chaos, while the rest of us failed by not taking a stand against their behavior. Many of us are so sorry about our lack of participa-tion; we should've protested the protests. We could've done this by standing up to, and resisting, people like Abbie Hoffman, Jane Fonda, Tom Hayden, and John Kerry. One example of a childish tantrum we could've resisted: Just think of the university "sit-ins" of the late '60s.[8] Another example: We could've stood between the hippie protestors and the Vietnam soldiers who were coming home. That way the hip-pies' spit, bagged urine, and feces[9] would've landed on us instead of the soldiers. We should've done these things, but we didn't. We were too busy trying to be "decent." (And in weakness we thought that if the agitators were given some of that candy they were screaming for, they would shut up and go away.) So this book is being offered as a kind of penance -- even though it's more than 40 years too late.

And it's really too late for my high school classmate and friend, Lynn Palmer. The two things I heard him say about his Vietnam experience were: "Not a day goes by that I don't think about what happened," and "I just never got over how people could treat other people." I'm sorry, Lynn. I never told you that you were one of my heroes.

The Frisbees and the Milk Duds are siblings. They always go hand in hand. When you finish the first chapter you'll be up to speed on the concept.

In an effort to understand and then describe what is happening in our country, I've tried to be true to four foundational guidelines:

**One: *Call no man a fool.*** Christians assume the self-evident truth that mankind (i.e. every person) bears God's image. This truth has proven to be a historically powerful force. It helped form the bedrock of this country, and it was the primary motivating principle for monumental societal changes. Things like ending slavery and elevating the status of women.

The concept of God's image in man is a major obstacle in the path of modern social reformers. If God's image is indeed in man then arguments against issues like abortion and socialism are obvious and indisputable.

But the concept also presents a challenge to the social reformers' antagonists -- in other words to people like me -- as books like this attempt to expose and refute the social reformer's ideology. The temptation in writing is to take the easy route and call these people "fools." I'm going to try to avoid doing that, but it's a difficult task because there's a lot of foolish behavior going on. It will require some discernment by the readers, but hopefully they will appreciate the painstaking effort trying to call out *foolish behavior* without calling anyone a *fool* – trying to simply identify folly. Sort of like *"Love the sinner, but hate the sin."* Am I wrong here? That is a God-like characteristic, isn't it – to hate sin? Is that not worthy of emulation? Unfortunately, in our current cultural context where a lot of people think they *are* what they *do*, this is a difficult, and perhaps impossible, distinction for many to make.

(I will however, frequently use the term "indecent" to describe those who act indecently. Admittedly, this is utilizing the author's bully pulpit. Try to think of it as convention more than a judgment.)

Let's get hypothetical and try to illustrate this challenge of addressing behavior and not the person. Let's say you're the parent of a 12-year old. You are completely committed to providing opportunities for this child to get educated, stay healthy, mature socially, and gracefully find his way into the modern world. While doing these things you are also trying to help him find his own identity. But it's getting harder for you to do all of this. Your child has been coming under increasing influence from a group of kids at school who are known for being anti-social and rebellious. And one morning he shows up at the breakfast table wearing all black, sporting dark eyeliner, and his once blond beautiful hair is spiked and dyed jet-black. What do you do?

My wife has a wise suggestion. Simply tell your son there will be no breakfast until the real son shows up.

I know that many of my friends did similar things with their children in similar situations. For the most part, their efforts failed. I also know what these parents didn't do. It's something that I think should be considered. Will someone please try this: Have a fit of hysterical laughter so vicious that you collapse on the floor.

So now the reader knows the approach this book is taking. It's going to try to ridicule what's ridiculous.

**Two: *Avoid reacting to feelings.*** There's a lot of discussion today about where culture is headed. Too many ideas begin with phrases like "one feels....", or "there is a sense that......" etc. I think you get the idea. But if you don't, just go back and listen to the aforementioned Dr. Emma Russell. It's sad, but true: many articles and books work from feelings at the expense of reasoned arguments and factual references. Also, we have reached a point where today's subjective feelings often dictate the "facts" of factual past events. History is being revised,[10] hourly, and one driving force is a desire to protect the self-esteem of people who've been labeled "weak" or "disadvantaged." It's utterly insane. And, furthermore:

> *Those who cannot remember the past are condemned to repeat it.* (George Santayana and Edmund Burke)

So now we find ourselves on the path to condemnation, because it's impossible to understand history's effect on culture while having a phobia about facts. In other words, it's impossible to remember the past if the real past has been either erased from memory or overwritten with lies. That last sentence is about as airtight and simple a statement as I've ever written; who could argue that it's wrong?

Contrast that loose approach to history with what you find here. I'm not really sure about all the meaning inherent in this contrast – I'm a literal thinker, not a fact-o-phobe -- so I'll leave it to the reader to dwell upon the differences. Suffice it to say that you won't find within these pages any appeal to feelings as the basis for developing informed ideas about certain key events in America's history. There are, however, two exceptions:

> Exception #1: I'm making a concession to cultural ambiguity by frequently appealing to Wikipedia[11] as a sourcing tool. This is an awful, but necessary compromise. It's necessary because internet informational sites have become the language *du jour*. But here's why it's awful: We noted that Wikipedia is continually being revised. These revisions come from people who are filtering ideas and events through personal experiences and prejudicial world views. Granted,

every world view is prejudicial, and granted, history has always been told this way to some degree. For example, for 450 years Columbus was presented as the first European to set foot in the New World. His story was written in some cases, perhaps, by people with a prideful, nationalistic, or racial stake in his accomplishments. But it's absolutely essential that we understand his story was probably all the authors knew. They weren't privy to evidence of Norse settlements in Newfoundland that remained unknown until 1961. That kind of process – of being true to what is known at the time of writing – held sway at least in principle for 3000 years.

But now it's different. Radically different. It's as if we're on another planet. The dominant filters today are things like "political correctness" along with a desire to protect or enhance other's "self-esteem." These are mixed in with postmodern relativism. What results is a recipe for disaster for Western Civilization (see Burke and Santayana). These modern filters are far more hostile to truth than the pride of an obscure Spanish or Italian historian was back in the 15th and 16th centuries. Today we find that Wikipedia often seeks to force the future into a progressive, secular, utopian mold. It tries to do this by attempting to re-create the past as its editors promote lies while selectively filtering factual inputs. See the footnote example.[12]

Exception #2: The effort to not be influenced by feelings was only 99% successful. Page 63 reveals the gut-wrenching anguish we should all feel about the legacy of indecency we're leaving for our children. (But even in this case our feelings should drive us toward solutions, and solutions should work logically from facts.) So this is only sort of an apology.

**Three***: **Spin is a legitimate, effective tool.** The wary reader will notice a lot of spin. Spin can work two ways. Using an analogy, it can spin a baseball into the strike zone or out of it. Similarly, spin can expose and enhance the truth, or it can obscure truth while producing confusion. Obviously I wouldn't have played this card face up unless the mantra in this book was to get at reality. You be the judge, but please note that there is fact-seeking spin aiming at what is real, and there is fact-obscuring spin which can deviously drive us into the fog of uncertainty, or even untruth. One big clue about the foundation for much of this discussion is the volume of footnotes at the end of the book.

Terminology manipulation is a form of spin. And it's used nefariously by the Left. This will be discussed at length at the proper point in the book. The reader needs to be warned at this point that a lot of words and phrases will appear in quotations or parentheses. It's normal to do this some, but there's way more than normal here. There's a reason for this. The discourse about social changes is in the process of being hijacked by agitators who are either changing the meaning of some words or creating new words or phrases. Two examples of new phrases are "politically correct" and "civil disobedience." I, for one, refuse to legitimize the false premises of the social reformers. As a result, these terms will be treated as outcasts from the common language and left inside quotations. So please bear with the profusion of quoted words and phrases.

Additionally, photo shopping is also a form of spin. There's a lot of photo shopping in this book. But it all happens on only two photos. Pages 39 and 85. All the rest are the real deal.

**Four: *Polarization is absolutely necessary.*** Polarization is apparently an unavoidable by-product of clarity. One way postmodern thinking has facilitated decline is by calling everything "gray" instead of accepting that a lot of things are "black and white". Or to say everything's relative, with no absolutes. Example: some have, just by the process of thinking, painted themselves so deep into irrationality that they're no longer able to call Communism "evil." Clarifying the issues drags us away from that kind of wimpiness and is therefore necessarily polarizing. And if there are scoundrels involved, it drags them out into the light.[13] I hope this book polarizes in a way conducive to making truth clear, and choices obvious.

So that's the game plan. My desire is to use respect, facts, spin, and polarization in ways that promote a broader perspective of where we're from, where we are, and where we're headed. I invite you to read this, be polarized, and then either throw it in the trash or pass it on. And remember: Under the current cultural standards for what-is-real, I claim 100% accuracy for every word, every thought recorded on these pages. According to these ridiculous (yet accepted) standards, if it's what I feel, then it's as true as anybody else's "reality."

**Disclaimer:** America today is a cultural battleground. And progressives tell us this war is being waged on behalf of a group of people -- the "disadvantaged." This group includes women, minorities, LGBTs, and others. But primarily in our country for the past 50 years, the focus has been on Americans of African descent. Thus it should come as no surprise to the reader that a lot of the focus in the following pages will fall upon that segment of American society.

This book takes issue with the idea that what the progressives are doing is "on behalf" of the disadvantaged. I believe that too many changes are happening at their *expense*. These groups are paying for the Left's destruction of Western Culture with their loss of dignity, loss of self-sufficiency, and loss of opportunity. This assessment of what is going on around us is argued for frankly and without apology. And it's done frequently through the use of satire.

So that brings us to the disclaimer: The author is totally committed to the belief that every human being, regardless of race, ethnicity, or gender, is absolutely equal in the eyes of our Creator and should thus be equal in the eyes of every other human being. If anyone thinks they're reading something that in any way supports ridicule of someone's personhood, they have totally misunderstood what is being said. In other words, the redneck racists and homophobes who think they may have found fuel for their hatred of their fellow man have totally missed the intentions of the author. It requires a certain amount of intelligence to grasp the following concept, but it has to be stated again: There may be ridiculous human behavior, but there are no ridiculous human beings.

# *Prologue:* Lofty Thoughts

Lofty thoughts seem to come easy for me. Easier than for most folks anyway. Haven't yet figured out why this is, but I'm working on it. Sometimes when I'm up front, flying this big Airbus A300 jet, the answer seems right there on the edge of consciousness.

The job looks glamorous on paper, but in reality it's not. Physics professor Dr. Art Dowell warned that my chosen career would basically be just glorified truck diving. He was right to a certain degree. But knowing now what I didn't know then, I still would've chosen the same path. It's not like I *wish I didn't know now what I didn't know then*[14]........ or something like that. And speaking of Bob Seger, I sometimes feel his pain:

> On a long and lonesome highway,
> > East of Omaha.
> You can listen to the engine
> > Moaning out its one lone song
> You can think about the woman,
> > Or the girl you knew the night before.
>
> But your thoughts will soon be wandering,
> > The way they always do.

When you're riding sixteen hours
   And there's nothing much to do
And you don't feel much like riding,
   You just wish the trip was through.

Say, here I am, on the road again.
   There I am, up on the stage.
   Here I go, playing star again.
   There I go, turn the page.[15]

Turn the page and here we go again, driving the jet from Paris Charles de Gaul, to Vienna, to Budapest. Maybe one day I'll figure out what's lofty about all this, but for now I just have to accept that it's a special gift to be able to wander, and wonder, all over Europe for two weeks each month.

Tonight's flight is typical. Or maybe it's today's; I dunno anymore. The flight preparation begins at 2am on the airport ramp in CDG after leaving the hotel at midnight -- Is that last night, yesterday, or today??? No time to dwell on it, 'cause things are hopping; chaotic actually. There's only 30 minutes to:

    Load freight_____
    Sign paperwork_____
    Get clearance_____
    Check the clearance_____
    Load navigation data_____
    Check the flight plan_____
    Security Brief_____
    Performance Brief_____
    Departure Brief_____
    "T" Brief_____
    Before Start checklist_____
    Start engines_____
    Cleared to taxi _____
    Configure the big jet_____
    Before Takeoff checklist_____

Cleared for Takeoff_____
Power up the engines_____
"80 knots"_____
"V1"_____


And then your first officer says: "Rotate." At this carefully calculated instant you pull slowly back on the controls. (5 seconds to pitch up to 18 degrees, and careful -- don't scrape the tail.) And then you get to participate a modern miracle as 180,000 pounds of metal, holding 50,000 pounds of fuel, and carrying 100,000 pounds of teddy bears and iPads and documents and pharmaceuticals and who knows what else accelerates from 0 to 160 in 10 seconds. And then the whole freaking contraption launches into thin air. *You're a (bloody) Airbus Captain; is there anything better in the world?*[16]   Wow!

Right after takeoff, and during initial climb, it gets even busier. It will get busy again for arrival and landing. In between there's little to do except reflect on some event or person or passion of your choosing. Several times each trip you and your copilot will solve all the problems of all the people in all the world.

On the road again, and one hour into this flight you realize for the ten thousandth time: *We're not in Kansas anymore.*[17] If your copilot is new and needs some hazing, you turn to him and say "*Toto, we're not in Kansas anymore.*" No, we're not........... We're 35,000 feet above the Austrian Alps. Oops, wrong movie; this one's *The Sound of Music.*

A German city slides by, below and to the left. It's Munich. And down there somewhere in the confusion of lights is another actor in our play. A young (probably) blond man is watching our blip, FDX 5212, crawl across his radar scope. We address him as "Munchen Control." Working in a dark, windowless room, he is now looking through sleepy 4am eyes at a nearly empty radar display. He has almost nothing to do. There is so little talk on the radio that my copilot and I worry our radios may have failed. "Munchen Control, This is FedEx 5212, uh, you still there?" "FedEx, I have you loud and clear." The otherwise quiet interlude releases us to our thoughts.

Eastbound into a spectacular dawn. It's beautiful. No, it's *incredibly* beautiful, and the outrageous explosion of color draws silent praise from your heart for the creative intelligent power that made all this. But even this view, with its moment of grateful praise, is not enough to overcome back-side-of-the-clock fatigue. You're sleepy. And frankly a little bored. Your copilot is catching a quick nap, so you try to engage the mind by playing some games with the navigation computers. One of the games is "Where are we?" Press one of those little buttons and the display says

> *47 degrees 48' 12" North*
> *12 degrees 02' 41" East*

Did that answer do anything for you? It didn't for me either. Get some new rules: This time ask "Where are we from *where*?" You enter the letters "MEM" and it says we're 5017 miles from Memphis, TN. Put in "MHH" and it dutifully reports 4894 miles from your sailboat, which is swinging on a mooring in Hope Town harbor, Abaco, Bahamas. You enter

> *39 degrees 28' 12" North*
> *106 degrees 10' 23" West*

.......and it says 5292 miles from the top of "S" lift at Copper Mountain, Colorado. The distance here is more than just mileage, 'cause the name of the lift was recently changed to "Sierra." And your lungs have been compromised so you're not ever going back to ski off the top of that 12000' peak into the glorious soft powder on the north face of Union Peak. In this case, it's not the miles, it's the years.[18]

You're playing the simplest of games on the most expensive of consoles and it's engrossing for all of 5 minutes. Surely there's more meaning to life than this? OK.......try one more ....... type in the letters "LGAV." There's the usual 2 second pause, and then the display says Athens,

Greece is 877 miles over there, past your right wing tip. Now *there's* a reference point if there ever was one. And this one tells you where you really are in so many ways. Too many ways for this short book. You open up the coffee thermos, pour a cup, and let the caffeine do its magic. And then you begin to think; to think about the flow of Western culture that matured in the Athenian mind and then moved Westward. Westward like this ever brightening promise of a coming sunrise.

Greece's advancing light didn't fare well when it pushed south. There was some synthesizing with Egypt, but the Sahara proved formidable. Greece was gone for 1500 years when England, Belgium, Portugal, Italy and others approached sub-Sahara Africa from the sea, trying to colonize what was known to them as the "Dark Continent." A couple of decades, or a hundred or so years, and their influence disappeared from most African colonies. Only South Africa still holds to a workable version of Westernization. Will it last? Or will South Africa go the way of Rhodesia?[19]

Despite Alexander the Great and the later Marco Polo, Western culture also never made much of an Eastward impact. It left crumbling marble ruins in Anatolia[20] and the Levant.[21] It could not penetrate the Khyber Pass. England approached the Indian sub-continent from the sea, gained a foothold, but then retreated. India is pretty much back to being India, even though they do still have cricket. Australia and New Zealand remain civilized to varying degrees in the Western model. Ditto to a lesser degree in Singapore. In another fifty years we'll know who won the influence struggle between Britannia and China in Hong Kong. It looks like China herself, though flirting lately with capitalism, will probably remain relatively untouched.

But these forays were nothing compared to the way Greek ideas moved West through Europe to reach out and form new countries all the way across the Atlantic. The sun's up in our faces now and our "light" metaphor is approaching overexposure. So let's get another metaphor. Western culture flowed like *life blood* through Europe, across the Atlantic to permanently (perhaps) establish itself in South, Central, and North America. Portugal found Brazil. Spain influenced most of the remainder of South and Central America. France established itself alongside the British in Canada. The important note for us is that England established a small beachhead in the northeastern corner of the New World. It was from this beachhead that Western culture reached out and infused the English colonies with ideas, ingenuity, and energy.

In 1776 the colonies declared themselves free. 200 years passed, and all that America became bore down on a clueless Southern white boy from Columbus, Mississippi, who is still, to this day, awkwardly trying to make sense of his place in this big, wide world. That would be me. As a somewhat corrupted (and barely educated) product of 2600[22] years of simmering ideas born in the ancient Athenian Agora, I had to write this book. But I still can't figure out that lofty thought thing.

So Greece provided the world a new way of thinking. Then Rome built a homogenous empire. And Christianity spread through that empire, teaching moral accountability, a different kind of service, and an impossibly idealistic moral code. Rome, in the name of the Holy Mother, co-opted Christianity, venerated Mary, and mishandled the church's stewardship into a millennium of darkness. A thousand years, and then came Florence. Holland, France, and other countries along with Italy, were settings for a re-birth -- a Renaissance. And the Western story was painted in living color. About this time Martin Luther walked onto the stage and said "*Here I stand, I can do no other.*"[23] From here there was no turning back. The combination of Renaissance, Religion, and Western thought would prove over the next five centuries to be a formidable force.

Initially it was Spain that provided ships and funded early explorations. In 1588,[24] the British wrestled maritime dominance away from Spain. England took up the torch with more ships, mapped most of the known world, and defined and formalized freedom. It was in the English part of the New World where colonists fanned the Magna Carta's[25] ember into flames, paying with their own precious blood the price for the highest degree of secular freedom man has ever known.

In the two centuries following 1776, the Western idea of man's existence paid big dividends when it flowered in the fertile soil of the new
country. All was not perfect to be sure; it must be admitted that society
was far from decency with respect to racial issues. It must also be
admitted that 20th century efforts purportedly addressing these ills have
only made matters worse. More about this later. For the time being
what begs our consideration is this starting-point proposition: So far in
human history the 3 or 4 years either side of 1960 were about as good
as it gets. One of the by-products of Western thinking, both symp-
tomatic and symbolic of Western influence, was an otherwise unsuspecting bystander. Unsuspecting until the next chapter. It was the
American game called "baseball."

# 1   In The Big Inning

In the beginning there was baseball.  But it was only sort of in the beginning.  First there had to be Greece,

then Rome,
then Jesus,
then Rome-Jesus,
then Western Europe,
then Christopher Columbus,
then King George,
then the national anthem, and
*then* there was baseball.

(You had to have a
national anthem before
you could play baseball.)

Baseball became a big deal -- even for the little kids; especially for the little kids.  But it wasn't fun for everybody.  Back in 1960 there could only be 15 on a team, so 5 or 6 of the boys didn't make the cut and went home crying.  They felt really left out.  It wound up being a devastating blow to the 10-year-old male psyche.  Some never recovered.

Out under the lights 9 little boys played against 9 other little boys twice each week with the whole town watching and cheering. 6 boys on each team were on standby. Some never got in the game at all, but were happy just to "dress out" and sit on the bench. A few of the games were even on the radio. But it's crucial to note something right here about the baseball kids. They didn't care one whit about all the attention; they just wanted to play ball. They would play "Sand Lot" ball all day. If there were only two kids, they would play "Indian Ball." (I have no idea how this name could possibly be insulting. But, even though this was 30 years before "Political Correctness," I'd still advise keeping the name quiet. Otherwise, the whole country will have to chip in to come up with another increment of reparations.)

Our neighborhood's pick-up games happened mostly in the vacant lot between our house and the McCrarys' house. My dad offered $20 to any kid who could hit a baseball through Aunt Doris and Uncle Wade's picture window. It was in straight-away center field, about 210 feet from the plate. But it was under the carport awning. So the ball would have to bounce.

A couple of years either side of 1960 life was awesome for almost everyone. But not for little boys who didn't make the cut. For some reason, the whole point for these kids seemed to be the potential for getting a lot of attention. They didn't think it was fair, so they went over into a corner, curled up into the fetal position, and began to whine. Every fiber in their being was crying out *"Look at ME!!!! PLEASE?"* Then fate smiled on their misery, because this was the precise point in history where all the stars lined up and some outcast invented the Frisbee.

But the whining didn't go away. And an even bigger problem developed mostly because all the commotion interfered with baseball. The normal people were always in a hurry to get to the games, so they were like *"Will you please put those Milk Duds back and be quiet so I can pay for the Gatorade?"*[26] Sometimes the parents would finish the whole ugly scene with another "request." They'd say *".......or I'm gonna take this belt to your bottom."* The parents could get away with stuff like that back then. The whole town was in on it. For a while there the kids didn't have a chance. I know this is just wishful thinking, but if that's what people mean today by "It Takes a Village" then bring it on.

2

A few years went by. The whining got louder, and the town finally
became so bothered that they put
their belts back on and decided to
help the whiners build their own
Frisbee park.  Parents would drop
the Frisbee kids off at the Frisbee
park, go watch the baseball kids,
come back and pick up the Frisbee
kids and go home. At home the family would clip the box scores from
the local paper, while the Frisbee
throwers would go off into in their
corner and whine some more -- this
time about not being on the radio or
in the paper.

Of course the little girls were left out.  But most of the girls didn't want
to play anyway because there was no crying in baseball.[27]  They were
content to go off to learn music and twirling, and to practice for the next
Miss America pageant.

The contented girls were usually the cuter ones.  Sometimes they
would slip into a trance just looking at the little boys in their uniforms.
But some of the girls weren't content at all with the baseball boys getting most of the attention.  So they began to whine because *they'd* been
left out.  Erica Wilson was the most miserable and made sure everyone
knew it.  Her mother was Maud Wilson -- *The* Maud Wilson.  Of course
we all remember Maud:  She was the first woman in America to go to
a factory job just like the men.  It was a sure 'nuff 5-day-a-week job,
8 to 4, lunch pail and occasional time and a half overtime.  She even
made the covers of *Time* and *Life.* These magazines were ahead of the
cultural curve, reporting that she had been "liberated."  She was almost
the perfect poster-girl except she had no bras to burn.

Maud thought baseball was the reason her daughter was always so
unhappy.  Then all the stars lined up again and softball was redis-
covered.  But nobody came to the silly softball games.  Maud started

having weird, hazy dreams. Something about "Title 9" that she'd have to figure out later. Right now, though, she was just puzzled that no one came to see her daughter's games. And Maud never noticed the ironic fact that a disproportionate number of the girls on the softball field didn't look like normal girls. It sure was confusing, standing right there at the crossroads of American culture.

OK; I lied. It wasn't a crossroads; it was a fork. There was always a big crowd milling around at The Fork, trying to figure out what to do, where to go. These were the moderates. They always felt strongly both ways. And here before them were two road signs. One sign, pointing to the left, said "Weird," and the other sign, pointing to the right, said "Normal." Most people eventually chose to go to the right; these were the "*wierdophobes.*" Just a few went off to the left; these were the "*normalphobes.*" (Pay attention here, 'cause this is important. A *normalphobe* is someone who has a phobia about being normal.[28] Got it? And another important note: There's nothing wrong with throwing a Frisbee or playing softball. They're both great pastimes. What *is* wrong is generating legislation and court orders which attempt to force the normal segment of humanity into giving people in the shallow part of the Bell Curve[29] some feigned attention.)

After choosing a direction for life's journey at The Fork, there was no turning back. The First Baptist youth minister, Briley, went to the right. She said she thought she saw Maud and Erica disappear around the corner, heading off to the left. It was hard to be sure on account of Maud's really short hair and all the dirt on Erica's shabby jeans and t-shirt.

While some of the baseball kids enjoyed more and more winning seasons, the Frisbee throwers and the softball players had more and more whining sessions. They realized they were starting to gain some attention, and they decided to go public. And so "protests" were born. The "protests" were where these misfits turned into "agitators." (But the terms "protest" and "agitators" proved too accurate and descriptive, so the whiners went into the stealth mode and became "organizers.")

The whiners couldn't go home after the (protests), so they would get together over at the Wilsons' and read about themselves in the paper and save the clippings. At first the reports were rather negative. (We're being charitable here -- "scathing" would be a better word.) This was the precise point in history where someone invented the "breakout session." Breakout sessions are where small groups of people sit around tables and pool their ignorance.[30] They had lots of these sessions, mostly whining about being left out and saying things like "You don't know what it's like to be me!" Soon they convinced themselves it was better to be hated than ignored. And after they crossed that threshold, none of them had any trouble anymore coming to grips with publicly acting like an idiot.

For lack of a better year, it can be argued that 1960 marked a cultural dividing point for America. After that year, over here on the right you had baseball players, cheerleaders, and piano players. And on the left were the softball players, Frisbee throwers, and (protesters). These two distinct camps were forming in the historical context of anti-American sentiment that pre-dates the author's personal experience, and thus pre-dates the entry point of our discussion in this book. Hatred by radicals toward the "establishment" had begun to coalesce over a decade earlier as actors and activists were backed into a corner by Congress and refused to renounce communism. So by 1960 the anti-Western Culture movement had been simmering for at least a decade. It may be helpful to think of 1950 as an undersea earthquake, with the early '60s swelling up with the first visible signs of a rising tsunami. America has subsequently been battered by stronger and stronger waves of destruction from the Left. These waves have surfaced in both Republican and Democrat administrations.[31] However, the stronger impacts have come in the Johnson, Carter, Clinton, and Obama regimes. The years 2008 through 2010 saw the worst destruction. It's possible that we may have weathered the storm. It's also possible that the next wave will produce total devastation. And it may be the height of naiveté to believe that it still could go either way.

As we're about to see, the decade following 1960 would provide more wedge issues, driving the baseball kids and the Frisbee throwers further and further apart. But before this could happen, the discontented normalphobes wanted a voice, a place at the table. They were dying to "be somebody." The vehicle for accomplishing this came to be known as "The Chattering Class."

# 2 Classless Chattering Class

When nobody's paying any attention, some people go get a meg-
aphone.  And then they use it to make some really loud obnoxious
noises.  The main operating principle for scoundrels may be this: *The
squeaky wheel gets the grease.*

If whining children never mature, they grow up to be whining adults.
*If* they grow up.  As we'll see in chapter 4, it's not prudent to assume
everyone will become adults.  But before we get to that discussion we
need to take a look at where a lot of today's professors, actors, media
personnel, politicians, wordsmithers came from.  And I forgot to mention an ever growing chunk of religious leaders.  One really smart person called this conglomeration of agitators the "Chattering Class," but
he was quick to point out they were, and still are, classless.  He said
that many of them were just a bunch of slouching, wandering poets.[32]
These people talked a lot and tried to come up with some ideas that
would validate their significance.  But all the good ideas had already
been taken.  So they came up with some rogue ideas.  Other than that,
they produced nothing of any use or practical value.

Somewhere in here one of them had the sinister idea that if they could
control the public discourse, they could feel important and gain some
closure.  So they went to work integrating their whining into the media
and began to push culture away from common decency.  The effort was

effective, accomplishing results that are way out of proportion to their numbers. Looking at the results from four decades of disproportionate influence, we now can see (for example, in the picture below) that the end result is somewhere around one thousand per cent degeneres.

Whoops, I meant *degenerate*. But here's how it went down: The normal people worked real hard and produced such a robust economy that there were too many jobs. It had to happen: one of the classless, shiftless Frisbee throwers was the only wordsmithing applicant at a brand new newspaper. So of course

he got hired. And this was hard to figure: He started railing against the free market in his editorials. The paper dithered around for a while, but finally admitted they got a lemon. They wanted to let him go, but by then they'd been unionized. Unionization served a good purpose once, when it worked to solve the problem of abuse. But having solved that problem, unions have gone on to create some unnecessary chaos. Parenthetically, I'll spend three little paragraphs right here describing what that last sentence means.

Some company owners and officers are greedy. They want to make more and more money. Sometimes they do unethical or criminal things to get the dough. But it bears remembering that their greed has a vested interest in seeing the company, the cash cow, continue to function and function well.

Some company workers are also greedy. But their greed is different. In many cases they are greedy for recognition. There is a built-in human resistance which produces discontent while serving at the behest of another person. (Never mind that serving someone else is necessary in order for most of us to make a living.) Playing off this discontent, unions can, and often do, coerce companies into concessions. The concessions frequently create an environment where the worker can tell his boss where to go, and do it with impunity. I guess this was the kind of situation one of my co-pilots was arguing for when he got all red-faced and started pounding his fist on the airplane's glare shield. Why are you doing this, Wayne? *All I want is some respect!*

The point in the Management/Labor contrast is this: One side of the divide wants the company to financially succeed while the other tends to default to the point where it could care less. The industry scuttlebutt about Pan Am Airlines going out of existence says that the motto of many of the entrenched employees was "100% pay until the very last day." Their point was what?

OK, that foray into labor philosophy was a little weird. But it's important because of the influence labor relations have had on the decline of America. The practical bottom line is that many unions have tragically evolved into overweight bureaucracies seeking to perpetuate them-selves. Somewhere in their evolution many of them have lost their legitimate reason for being. From that loss of purpose moment onward, America has found herself committed to less-than-mediocre. Playing the union card is proving to generally be part of a downward, dead-end spiral that always seems to end in bankruptcy.

Now back to the rise of the Chattering Class. Another one of the nor-malphobes went to work as a newscaster. He was Nathaniel Watson, Jr., who majored in art, had painfully precise diction, and whose dad, Nat (Sr) owned the TV station.[33] Nat hoped his son would grow up to be normal. But Nathaniel was odd. He craved attention, and figured out he could control people for almost ten seconds by insisting every-one use four syllables when speaking his name. Four seconds to think about it, two to say "*Na~than'~ee~uhl*", and then four more to reflect on how weird the whole experience was. 4+2+4=10. But I digress -- the bottom line was this: These two Frisbee throwers defaulted into the media just as the American form of Western Culture was nearing its peak in the early 1960's. The peak came later in the decade, and it

9

was all downhill from there. (There must be some curiosity here about where this "peak" actually occurred. It was the exact moment Neil Armstrong's foot touched the Moon's surface.)

So again we see that as American culture was approaching a zenith, there were beginning to be two parallel subcultures. There was the Frisbee world and the baseball world. In the baseball world, the players still just wanted to play baseball. Some of the older players were becoming more famous and getting richer and playing on national TV. They were buying big houses and big cars and signing autographs and flying around in airplanes all over the place. There was Mickey Mantle, number 7, and Roger Maris, number 9.

In the Frisbee world the whiners were beginning to force their way onto the public stage and were thus taking a foothold in the American media. You had people like Na~than'~ee~uhl, Erica and Maud, and an ever growing number of wordsmithers. These people mistakenly thought the world revolved around the baseball players. They began creating lives and careers that would work to make the world revolve around them. And that was how it began.

# 3  Good Morning Vietnam!

You may have noticed that while the normal kids were playing base-ball, and the normalphobes were infiltrating culture, there was a war going on.  Russian Communists were trying to take over the earth to either "bury"[34] us or else make everybody peasants. This meant all the women in the world would have to wear those drab kerchiefs that only come in brown or gray or black.  The thought was horrifying to the decent people, so they began looking for a time and place to make a stand.  The time was August 2, 1964.[35]  The place was Vietnam. America was there in Vietnam because the French had messed things up terribly.  That brings us to another slight detour to get some historical perspective.  It might seem tedious at first, so just dig in with me for six short paragraphs and hang on.

Near as anybody can tell, Southeast Asia was colonized by France in 1860 and became French Indochina.  Everything was OK (if owning a colony -- hegemony – was your kind of thing) for about 80 years. But in 1940, France ceased to be a country when Hitler walked up the Champs-Elysees and saluted the adoring French masses with the four middle fingers of his right hand.  It was at that moment that Vietnam was separated from its sponsor.

One year went by.  Pearl Harbor was attacked, and now the whole free world was in a fight for its very existence against the first Axis of Evil.[36] That would be Germany and Italy, and around here on the other side of the globe, Japan. So the Allies found themselves in Vietnam trying to hold off the imperialist Japanese. The downside of being part of the "Allies" was that you had to pretend the Communist Russians were decent human beings. Most of the collateral damage in the aftermath of WWII was because the Soviets leveraged a lot of bloodshed to get a seat on the world stage.

Japan finally surrendered. What happened next in Vietnam was called a "leadership vacuum," but that's a misnomer because there were leaders of every stripe and color running around everywhere trying to stake out territory. Technically, the victors in WWII agreed to give Vietnam back to the French.[37] It was sort of a "Gentleman's agreement." But you know the Russians and the Chinese -- they always cross their fingers every time they're asked to be "gentlemen."

A struggle ensued and went on for the next 30 years. Initially the struggle was between the imperialistic interests of the French and the imperialistic interests of the Communists. The French were insisting that Indochina was theirs by right. Guess you could say "Rightfully so!" But things got a little too hot, and -- you know the French -- they just packed up their things and slinked out of town in the middle of the night.[38] The US took up the slackers' slack, and tried to hold off the Communists. The US, with almost zero colonial interest, was trying to *prevent* imperialism. That's a big distinction. What would've happened if the US had won? Take a look at Japan, or Germany, or Italy. America has proven herself again and again in the past century to be anti-imperialistic.[39]

There are two ways to accomplish imperialism: Territorially, from without; and ideologically, from within. The French fought *for* imperialism territorially. Then the US followed them and began fighting the war *against* imperialism. Still primarily in terms of territory. The Communist were fighting for imperialism primarily from within. And not just north and south of the DMZ.[40] One way they did this was to cultivate some willing comrades in the US chattering class, and then use these puppets to take the war to US soil.[41] America was right about the enemy, but she was wrong about the battlefield.  It was on a whole 'nother continent.

So while the decent Americans were thinking they were fighting Communism way over there, it slowly began to dawn on them in the late '60s that the real battle against Communism was going on right here at home.  The key battles were fought at what should've been serene academic institutions.  Places like Kent State, Berkeley, Madison, Harvard and Columbia.  Immature, long haired activists squeezed some candy, kicked and screamed, and turned the universities into unregulated social laboratories.  Regular folks finally started waking up, but it was too late.  The home front revelation came as a shock, because people who are decent and hate evil never seem to get spooled up for the battle until hits them in the face.[42]  Think of it like this: There's just no conceivable way anyone could anticipate that Barbarella, the bimbo astronaut,[43] would sneak up through our pacifist Left flank and destroy our country's resolve from within.

Here's some more info from another angle about the home front conflict.  Up until the decline-of-American-culture, news media and movies always showed soldiers as normal people who acted courageously and were heroic.[44]  For a few years in the early '60s, that's the way things went with Vietnam.

Steve Canyon and Buz Sawyer were two of the soldier heroes portrayed in comic books and comic strips from World War II through Vietnam.

But things changed, and it all happened in such a subtle way that most people didn't see it coming. About 100,000 Frisbee throwers[45] were away on 10-year vacations in Canada, or off to egg-head schools in Europe with Bill Clinton. (The ones in Canada made too clean a break, and couldn't figure out how to come home until Jimmy Carter[46] fixed everything in 1977.) Even though they were away they still couldn't stand it that the soldiers were getting all the attention back home in America. So they got together with movie directors like Stanley Kubrick, Francis Coppola and Oliver Stone, and produced some propaganda. Films like Dr. Strangelove, Apocalypse Now, and Born on the Fourth of July. This essentially changed the paradigm. Suddenly, and I do mean suddenly, we started hearing about cowardly soldier-goats and brave deserter-heroes. John Kerry saw the shift coming, couldn't find his spine, and decided to throw away his medals so he could throw in with the new "heroes." The tipping point for this changeover happened while I was doing homework for Mrs. Sutton's 4th period chemistry class way back in the 11th grade. 6:25PM Central Standard Time, February 27, 1968.[47]

So the papers began bending the news into dark tragedies. And the wandering poets shouted a bunch of F-words.[48] And the hippies who were still at home put up a bunch of tents in Seattle and San Francisco, and started spitting on the soldiers. Then Walter Cronic showed his colors. And Vietnam became a political war. And Dan Rather disrespected Nixon, and the country lost its nerve, and then the president backed down. Isn't it amazing how much damage a group of screaming adolescents can do at the grocery check-out? Now there are some Frisbee-throwing wordsmiths whose only purpose in life is to make sure everyone thinks Lyndon Johnson's Democrat war was Richard Nixon's Republican war, and was a total waste. I don't know, maybe it's just me, but I caught a TV travelogue about Vietnam the other day, and it looked like the communists were all gone. Also, you may have heard that in 1989 that stinking wall was beat to rubble,[49] so maybe Southeast Asia was just one battle in a larger war. History will tell, but only if Oliver Stone doesn't write the history. (Dan Rather won't be writing it though, 'cause CBS said "We'd Rather ...not!"[50])

We're talking about spin here.  And the mainstream media's spin about the real heroes -- the soldiers -- is unconscionable.  (But, then again, who has a conscience?)  Sadly, the spin continues today and will continue, I guess, as long as we have the Chattering Class.  Example: During the Iraq war we had to painfully endure the never ending story of Cindy-Sheehan-in-the-ditch.  Even though her viewpoint represented less that about 1% of military families' views, the Cindy-Sheehan-in-the-ditch story ran on the major networks for *months* in 2005.  It's debatable whether or not her story merited a place on the national news.  If it deserved any exposure at all, the story should've been told once and it should've lasted about 2 or 3 eye-blinks.  If Dan Rather was still at CBS he could have invested just one breath and said:

> *This is Cindy Sheehan.  Her son Casey was killed in Iraq.  She went crazy.  Now she lives in a ditch.  End of story.  Courage.*[51]

Ninety-nine % of the soldiers (including Casey Sheehan) and their families (not including Cindy) have stories that are heroic.  They're heroes just for signing up.  So why did we have to endlessly endure Cindy's pathetic excuse for human behavior?  When did it become acceptable for news outlets to have any agenda other than reality / truth?[52]  How can they get away with collaterally trashing the most heroic among us?

# 4 Woodstock (Not the Canary)

Vietnam exposed a generational flaw. Its influence and fallout took America a long way down a very bad road. But that war wasn't the only venue for human cowardice and indecency. We need to slip back and look at other important factors. So we go back again to the '60s.

It was late in the decade when something tragic happened to the human race. For the first time in history a large section of a whole generation failed to make it through puberty. Consequently, the Frisbee throwers and the softball girls didn't come out the other side of adolescence as adults. They became hippies, discovered marijuana, and slid all the way down to rock bottom. Rock bottom may have lasted about a week in August, 1969. That was when 500,000 of these people gathered at Yasgar's farm for a defining event called "Woodstock."

It was a week when it was OK to reproduce Sodom and Gomorrah against the backdrop of some of the greatest music of the time. If you kept your eyes closed at Woodstock and listened only to the performances, everything was just fine. But if you opened your eyes you could see that things were mostly muddy, and really obscene and decadent. And unfortunately, you had to hear more than just the performances. Like 5-year olds on steroids the participants cheered real loud every time someone shouted the F-word.

And then there was the weather: Frequent lightning, ominous thunder and buckets of rain. Seizing the moment, the hippies got high on drugs, got out of their clothes, and got it on in the mud, wrestling with multiple partners. It became a sobering experience when the drugs wore off. That's when they rinsed clean and tried to figure out what the heck had just happened. Only two choices: *(1)* Admit they acted like total fools, or *(2)* pretend there is *no-such-thing-as-morality.* Cowardice prevailed; they chose *no-such-thing-as-morality.*

And then something happened that was incredible, unbelievable and utterly galling. It was *breathtaking.* At the same time they were saying *"There's no morality"* they were also saying *"We have the high moral ground."* So they started looking down their noses at the normal decent achievers. With contempt. With feigned *moral* indignation. I kid you not. Talk about chutzpah! It was sort of like *"If you're being run out of town, act like you're leading a parade."* Or maybe *"If you do something stupid, pretend you're a genius."* They never would have pulled it off except they now had the newspapers, TV, radio, universities, and most of the magazines. The media did their part by filtering most of the repulsive info out there about Woodstock. Now you look back and all you see is a parade. Decadence? What decadence? Bottom line for history: Even though the official "Summer of Love" was actually 1967, many people now recall Summer, 1969, as the "Summer of Love, Part 2." Either year, it doesn't really matter, does it? I mean, are we gonna operate under relativism or not? At any rate, the term "Summer of Love" sets the Gold Standard for revisionism. It's a warm fuzzy term sometimes applied to a 90-day period in 1969 "blessed" with mass fornication, indecency, drug use, and even mass murder.[53] Go figure.

Regrettably, Woodstock didn't just happen and then go away. It was part of a movement. One legacy that came out of this movement was cute bumper sticker slogans that tried to sum things up. The slogans were both clever and succinct. ("Sound bites" and "Purpose Statements" were thankfully still about 3 decades away.) Some of these sayings sounded real cool -- Like *"Question Everything."*[54] Turns out, however, this was only a partial quote. And borrowed from the Bible at that. Here's the whole quote: "Question everything -- *hold fast to that which is true."*[55] Guess they couldn't use the whole quote without committing intellectual suicide. You had to wait about ten more years if you needed to avoid consistency and absolute truth. Postmodernism to the rescue.

But something else they said proved totally pernicious and evil. They said *"If it feels good, do it!"* Now this kind of thinking, per se, wouldn't've been all that devastating in the long run, because it was inherently self-correcting (you know -- overdoses, AIDS, jealous lovers-with-a-gun, etc.). But not even the hippie who brain-farted this saying could fore-see the coming horror: His cute little phrase morphed into judicial phi-losophy. America had tediously built up two full centuries of proven impartial Law and blind Justice. Now these time-proven principles have to take a back seat to "wise Latina"[56] experiences and subjec-tive constitutional interpretations. The stated goal of these interpreta-tions is called "social justice," which is really only anti-justice. And now we have too many crucial decisions being made by Liberals who are answering primarily to their feelings. Throw in the fact that a lot of these judges are obsessively normalphobic and Christophobic, and you can see right off that the decent people are facing a serious problem. And the problem we're facing is this: *They're using the judicial system to rule the Constitution unconstitutional.*

Here's something only slightly related. It's another example of how these quips can get out of hand real quick. Listen to Andre' Agassi -- he said *"Image is everything."* That's fairly benign when you're trying to sell SLR cameras. But it develops into the whole enchilada when campaigning for votes. Couple that mindset with no-requirement-for-voter-literacy and it's easy to see where this is headed. Now, which side was it that didn't want any kind of voter literacy test? Or maybe we should spin that last question for a little more polarizing clarity: Which side thrives on ignorance?

Let's not leave Woodstock just yet. Take one more look at those muddy fields. The symbolism is inescapable. Woodstock was a watershed event, pregnant with meaning. The quagmire illustrates perfectly the pitfalls of slippery-slope positions. For example: The wandering poets were inspired by the event, so they wrote and performed some simple

3-minute ditties about "The Age of Aquarius,"[57] about "Crystal Blue Persuasion,"[58] stuff like that. They got everybody thinking that Harmony and Understanding were just around the corner. That Sympathy and Trust would be abounding. That there would be no more Falsehoods or Derisions. That there would be Golden Living *Dreams of Visions.* Hold it right there -- stop the tape! *Dreams of Visions*????? Give me a break. Next thing you know someone will say something really stupid, like "*We are the ones we've been waiting for.*"[59]   Or maybe like "*I've been in 57 states - I think one left to go.*"[60]

They also sang "we've got to get ourselves back to the Garden."[61] And those of us who believed in God were suckered in. We thought they were making an allusion to the Garden of Eden. Now we know their allusion was only an illusion. And we know Steven Stills and Joni Mitchell were in cahoots with Darwin, trying to kill God. Turns out their garden was a jungle full of primates, with all of them just sitting around twiddling their opposing digits. The apes and monkeys were waiting, apparently, on the evolutionary clock. How could anyone sing about goin' back to *that* garden? We should all get some kind of refund.

# 5   Suicide of the Fittest

How convenient that we've just stumbled over the name Darwin.  But, then again, how could we avoid it?   A lot of the social changes we're talking about were pushed along with some help from an idea this man had about life.  That would be the *Theory of Evolution*.  Charles Darwin and his brother dreamed it all up way back in 1859.

Here's how it all happened: Charles and Eras had a bunch of fossils on the floor, along with a collection of drawings of finches and other birds.  Then the British Royal Society explorers came back from Africa with some sketchy information about monkeys and chimps and apes.  And over here on Charles' desk was a supply of opium.  All this stuff could neatly be arranged from the simple to the complex.  Amoebae down at the bottom.  Caucasians up at the top.  Opium in the Caucasians.  Or maybe the opium came first.

The whole set up was sitting there, staring the Darwins in their faces, and just begging them to conclude that life was evolving toward higher life-forms.  Voila' --- Evolution!

A lot of the thinkers began licking their lips.  They knew this new idea could be leveraged to accomplish two related things: One, banish God.  And two, exalt man.  Maybe then man could finally "be somebody."  (It seems so long ago, doesn't it -- The Tower of Babel?[62] That was

1600 BC, give or take a few months. Has it really taken us this long to recover?)

Problem was there weren't any fossils that showed the transitions. These missing fossils would've been what honorable scientists call "proof." So I guess that's where the word "theory" came in. People are still frantically searching all over the planet, and even on the moon and Mars, to find at least one of those billions and billions of transitional relics. They sure want to get rid of that pesky word "theory." A lot of them have all but given up, and just made up their own proof. You can see their "evidence" on the bumpers of about 18% of the Mini Coopers.[63] It's a fish with feet, and it looks like this:

But if you stand on your head, it's more accurate, 'cause it looks like this:

I dunno, postmodern scientists (oxymoron alert) may be able to "prove" anything they want to prove, but as for me and my house, we're sticking to the old paths. We're demanding that science be what it was when it produced Neil Armstrong's American footprint on the Moon: Science = demonstrable, measurable, and repeatable.[64] (Note to Barack Hussein Obama: We could not have walked on the Moon without American exceptionalism, ingenuity, and a free market economy. Note to Michelle: Now tell me one more time about how you've never been proud of your country.[65])

Anyway, the Darwins got all that stuff set up, neatly arranged in order of ascending complexity. And then Charles took another shot of opium and said "Let's see Eras, .........Let's put the black man right.......... in..........here!" In case you need a refresher course on Darwinism, "here" is somewhere between the monkeys and civilized white man. A few of the rest of their ideas may be worth considering, but only as long as we blind ourselves to their emphatically stated belief that Negroes are less evolved than Caucasians.

Despite the Darwins' bigoted, ignorant racial bias, evolution was making a pretty good run at capturing most scientific thinking. One reason is because it's a workable, practical hypothesis. In other words, even though it may or may not be true, it's descriptive enough to be useful. Examples: (1) Because of commonality between life forms, students can practice dissecting frogs, and then know something about what to expect when they grow up to be doctors and cut into human bodies. And (2) Similarly, drugs can be given to laboratory rats to provide predictable data for people. Sort of like this book: There may or may not be a conspiracy. But, the conspiracy context is useful as a tool to help describe and understand American decline.

Now this is all well and good up to a point, I guess. But then there were a couple of stupid human blunders late in the previous millennium that exposed the whole evolutionary facade. (Listen......hear that? Sounds like someone's saying "Don't pay attention to that man behind the curtain!") First, a big whale tried to swim up the Sacramento River *twice*,[66] leaving the salt and heading into fresh water. Humphrey the humpback was *twice* chased back through San Francisco Bay by a fleet of sonar-pinging boats. And then a couple dozen dolphins were discovered flipping around on a New Jersey beach.[67] About 22 or so Sierra Clubbers got together and worked night and day to shove them back into the ocean. Both human efforts failed to recognize this: The whale and the dolphins were going to be the next crucial chapters in species evolution. Humphrey was trying to convert to fresh water, and the dolphins wanted to become land mammals. So evolution, if it ever existed, ground to a whimpering halt all because of nearsighted human intervention. And now we're all sentenced to be the same for the next eon or maybe even 75 millions and billions of years or so. We've lost Carl Sagan, so we don't know the real figures anymore.[68] Regardless, it takes a long time for nature to regroup. Meanwhile, Darwin's theory is in suspension. Who would've thought the process was so fragile?

# 6   The Truth About SUVs

And while we're thinking about Sierra Clubbers, this is a good place to remember where SUVs came from.  During the '60s a lot of the hippies started pretending there was no God, and then couldn't figure out why there was this big hole in their hearts.  They were, like, so empty.  You can listen to songs like "I Am, I Said,"[69] "The Logical Song,"[70] and "Dust in the Wind"[71] and clearly understand their dilemma.  Their solution was to try to fill the void by worshipping nature.  (You know; Mother Nature / Mother Earth / The-Earth-Has-a-Temperature, that sort of stuff.)   So they put on their sandals and tie-dyed T-shirts, and proceeded to do lots of other stupid things like going deep into the wilderness to look at flowers and eat tree bark and sit cross-legged and hum.  There were a lot of problems with this, but the biggest was the fact that their psychedelic VW buses kept getting stuck in the mud.  This opened up a niche market for four-wheel-drive-all-terrain-vehicles. And the Jeep, with its military bloodlines, presented too much of an ethical hurdle for the Sierra Clubbers.  (This is what passes for a "moral dilemma" in the Frisbee world.)  So the capitalist free market came to the rescue when Toyota showed up with the Land Cruiser.  Everyone was happy and the SUV was a perfectly good vehicle until.............

.............. the stay-at-home moms, who had married the achievers, and who had given birth to  2.5 kids, figured out the obvious.  SUVs were perfect for shuttling kids back and forth to VBS and baseball and kids' birthday parties down at Chuck-e-Cheese.[72]   Fads usually spread like wildfire through the Garden Clubs, so almost overnight the suburbs were full of SUVs.  And now Sierra Clubbers can't say "SUV" on CNN without acting like they're vomiting.  It's their version of righteous indignation.  I don't know if you've noticed it yet, but vomit-simulation is their No. 1 method of responding to the facts.

While the hippies were still stunned from the shock of seeing Republicans driving *their* SUVs, the polar bear population was exploding.[73]  And somewhere in here a chattering-classless person got a picture of some polar bears enjoying a ride on a small ice block up north in the Arctic.

Now here I am trying to tell this convenient lie and it sure is inconvenient for me to have to admit the truth, isn't it?  I mean, it's obvious these bears were hibernating in a glacier.  And then a large chunk -- the chunk they were sleeping in -- broke off and began to melt in the incredibly warm Arctic waters.  And they can't swim to safety because of the decreased salinity.  Not enough buoyancy.  All this because my air conditioner uses HFC's[74] or CFC's.[75]  The chattering class actually expects us to believe this.  They must take Americans for a bunch of fools.

But wait a minute.......couldn't this be another evolutionary trial balloon? I think I can see *webbed feet.* And gills! We could be looking at the forerunners of the Great Northern Furry Bear-Fish! I mean after all, are we, or are we not, going along with Darwin's evolution thing? C'mon, man. Be non-linear......Think outside the box.

Anyway, the fake symbolism in pictures like this was used for propaganda by twisting it and milking it for about 5 gazillion dollars and Nobel Peace Prizes by shysters like AlGore. And to insure a lasting legacy of lies, pictures of similar scenes were woven into stories for children and distributed by the NEA. This may end up being the tipping point for human sanity. The little grade school kids -- our next generation -- are constantly being pushed to the edge. It was always tough enough trying to be a normal eight year-old third grader. Now these Ritalin saturated innocent

ones have to cope with latch-keys, single parents, sexual ambiguity,[76] two mommies, African history, Gay/Lesbian/Cross-Gender history, no morality, and 2+2=5. And here they're being forced to cry for the polar bears. Awww, those cute, sweet, cuddly polar bears.

**First:**
**Newsweek,** **April 28, 1975:**
(The Sky Is Falling -- It's getting Cold!)
**Then,**
**Newsweek,** **January 22, 1996:**
(The Sky Is Falling -- It's getting Warm!)
**Now,**
**Newsweek,** **May 28, 2010:**
(The Sky is Falling: Well,..... Just  Because.)

# 7  WTH?  YGTBKM!
(WHAT THE HECK?)    (YOU GOTTA BE KIDDING ME!)

Climate hysteria is an important cross-current in society. One essential element of this hysteria is complete-absence-of-Logic. People can't seem to figure out that feelings and science don't mix. Or that actors and science don't mix. And furthermore, a lot of people need to be reminded that real science is measurable and repeatable. And, here's a shocker: Facts don't change. (Wonder what the facts think about all this?) Today we have a lot of people who seem hell-bent on testing the limits of sanity. Characters like AlGore, DarylHannah, and Milhouse are acting like near-total lunatics. Or completely total lunatics. Like SherylCrow.[77]

Some scientists have abandoned any vestige of principle, gone political and put forth blatant lies. On the next page are a couple of simple graphs proving that AlGore's sensational "hockey stick" was based on *intentionally* misleading data. The odds of a conspiracy just went way up.

29

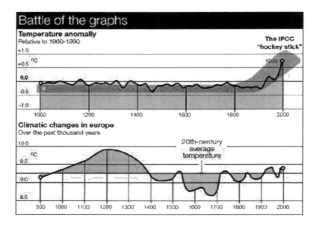

Here's another graph that suggests how much we've been duped. But don't take my word for it, do your own research.

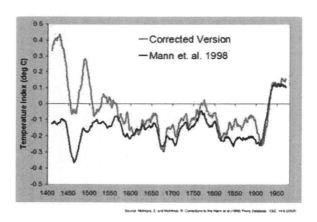

I wouldn't advise thinking about this, but if you inadvertently, involuntarily, accidentally find yourself dwelling on the thought of *President* Albert Gore, Jr., it won't be too long before you start praising God for the 8-year W blessing. BTW, W's Crawford, TX, ranch is rumored to have a carbon footprint of nearly zero. Hey.......Here's an idea: Let's circumvent the Main Stream Media, do some research, and find out for ourselves. Just go to google.com, type in "Geo. W Bush carbon footprint", and hit enter. (Better do it quick, before the revisionists get to the web.[78]) We will discover an inconvenient truth that really is true. And such fitting commentary on the differences between those who are busy chattering and those who are busy solving problems. It's also – through your participation -- a backhanded expose' of how media can selectively report "news" in order to prejudice the ever increasing number of non-literate voters. (The word "illiterate" seemed too damaging to some people's self-esteem, so I made up the less offensive word.)

But inserting the Green Script into recent history is superfluous. The God-fearing people had the simple, clear directive for environmental activism dumped in their lap thousands of years ago. I happened like this: God created humans, and their souls, as the crowning achievements of a 6-day project. Then He put them in charge. Told them to have dominion, to subdue[79] everything, to rotate their crops -- stuff like that. Then He gave out autographed User's Guides for the whole enterprise. The Guide shows that part of our job description is "Stewards of Creation." While we're at our assigned tasks -- picking up litter, treating animals humanely,[80] practicing selflessness, etc. -- we should also be constantly in prayerful awe of the power behind it all. The music of the spheres,[81] the changing of the seasons, the cycles of life: They all demand that we fall on our knees and praise Him with every fiber of our being. So.... I wonder..... I wonder if the Sierra Clubbers will send us a membership card?

# 8 Back to Baseball

Even with so many chattering agitators on TV, in newspapers and magazines, and in the movies, it was still a problem for the normalphobic Frisbee throwers that the biggest thing on TV was baseball. And I'm sure it can be easily documented from past data that there is a direct correlation between the number of self-validation counseling sessions and increased viewership during the World Series in late October. There was more whining, and it was even louder because of all that chattering. So the normal people who loved to watch Baseball, and twirl and play the piano tried one more time to make the whining go away. It was once again the classic wrong response to the screaming kid clutching those Milk Duds at the grocery check-out counter. The normal people said "Here, go have your own TV" and "Here, go have your own radio." Don't look now, but this is how the decent, hardworking people got to foot the bill for freeloaders like PBS, NPR, and Garrison Keillor. First they got their own Frisbee park, and then they got all this.

The agitators had already seized the self-proclaimed high *moral* ground back at Woodstock. Now they seized the self-proclaimed high *intellectual* ground. They did this, in one respect, by pretentiously naming their stations WKNO or WBIQ or WDIQ, etc. And by playing Mozart and Bach. And by broadcasting a lot of trivial trivia mental games seeking to highlight their own intelligence. It's all about who's intellectual. Just ask them.  Or listen to them: So many of their arguments end with the following *coup de grace* phrase "(these people) just don't get it."

Despite all this they were *still* whining.  Louder than ever.

About 40 years went by. decent folks forgot their lesson – again! -- let down their guard, and messed up big time.  In 2008 they said "Okay… okay…*OKAY!!!"* Here, go have a presidency."

This chapter was really, really short.  Don't get too cocky, cause the next one is really, really long.  It all comes out even in the end.

# 9 Got "Privilege"?

A while back in chapter 3 it was pointed out that the real heroes are the soldiers. And since I just mentioned that again, this would be the opportune moment to reintroduce myself. Never been a soldier. Been a hero, though. For 7 +/- people. Until they turned 8. Then I was just "Dad", or "Papa." It was great while it lasted.

Anyway, I was in a discussion the other day with an I-don't-see-how-we're-friends person. He's a Frisbee-thrower who has to take blood pressure medication every time he's confronted with the letters B-U-S-H. His reaction is reminiscent of what happens when someone holds a cross up to a vampire. We won't explore all the symbolism in that illustration at this point, but it sure is chock-full of meaning.

My friend can't seem to help joining in the chorus with other bleeding hearts when they trumpet that some of us don't understand the problems disadvantaged people face. They see me 60 years along on a journey, and think they can intelligently evaluate how I got here. Sometimes they try to create guilt by accusing people like me of being "winners of life's lottery."[82] But of course they're foolishly uninformed. And since I don't know what it's like to be them (as they adamantly say), then of course they don't know what it's like to be me. Or maybe we do know, but just don't know that we know. Who knows?

Since my friend broached the subject, some biographical facts are needed. Just between you and me, I'd be more than glad for everyone to experience life like I've experienced it. Here's what it's like to be me -- to be "advantaged" and "privileged":

You spend your first 5 years in what is basically a basement slum. You don't remember a lot about that, but you do have this feeling it was a real blast even though there was no air-conditioning. One memory lurks barely in the mind like an elusive dream: You're standing at the commode watching your mother rinse out one of your brother's three cloth diapers. The flush lever must be magnetized, because you see your hand reach for it and pull it down. *Kersploosh* -- The world's first disposable diaper! Just another tender mother and child moment.

In 1957 you move way out of town to a new house built by your dad when he used his accrued vacation from the Post Office. Took him about 6 months. The house is in your grandfather's old cow pasture and has small rooms, very little furniture and linoleum floors. No air-conditioning here either. If it starts raining during church, someone has to jump up and rush home to close the windows. And the laundry thing: If there's a thunderstorm with the clothes on the line, someone gets their face popped by the flapping sheets. Yet all these memories are pleasant: Sweet Summertime, Summertime.

You have one pair of shoes until you start playing sports, and then you have two. But that doesn't matter much because you go barefoot 90% of the time when not in school. (Remember those sand spurs?) No TV until about age 8; and then it's black and white, one snowy channel, rabbit ears + Reynolds Wrap. The cars your family uses are hand-me-downs with no air conditioner until you're about 16. You go thru K, then grade school, then high-school, then college with no air conditioner in the schools.  In college you live in a one-room attic "apartment" with one South-facing window and no air-conditioning. Did you get that?  In the South, in late Summer, in the attic, no air.

Jobs: Make some hamburgers (.90/hr), pound some concrete with a sledge hammer (1.20/hr), make some license plates (1.60/hr -- no kidding; in Mississippi the man I worked for underbid the penitentiary.  But then again, the ACLU probably wouldn't let the prisoners do it anyway.) You try to clean some commodes to help pay for college.  Take out a loan for the rest, and work for 15 years to finally pay it off.

After all that hard work, along with 16 years of formal education, you land your first real job.  It involves flying professionally as a corporate pilot, but it begins with two weeks of ditch-digging.  Shovel, blisters, dirt.

So that's it, up to about age 22.  Maybe there's a little "street cred" there?  And maybe you can get a feel for the plight of this working boy as he pounded away on a metal press in a sweltering windowless factory.  My words:

# Tag Poem

Said the Tag
    "I'll be myself!"
But the press proved
    to be the greater force,
And he became
    #47C 6741

The weight of conformity
    presses our souls
With patterned impressions
    of false reality.

And, like all the others,
    we become
Reflectorized images
    of someone else's butt.

I still have the original -- It's done in early magic marker on a vintage reflective steel plate. But enough of that. The point is that a lot of people are running around crying "You're privileged!" They have absolutely no clue what they're talking about.

So what do you think? Do you think my experience was common? Or was it rare? If it was common, then the bleeding hearts have a problem, because even the disadvantaged today have so much more than what was "privilege" for most of us. In other words, if we were "privileged", i.e. guilty as charged, how can anyone honestly argue that today's underprivileged have a right to more than my privilege? Don't they know they're already way ahead in the game? Don't get me wrong, I wouldn't change any part of my particular journey through life. (OK, I might have opted for braces.) It was all a blast and all a blessing.

BTW, the time has come to mention the things making some of us "privileged." It has nothing to do with luck, and it's not a lottery win. It has to do with a lot of hard work, discipline, persistence, and having a moral compass. I hope that the number of believers hasn't dwindled to the point where many people are offended as I give thanks here for my personal list of "blessings." Father *and* Mother. Family. Discipline. Church. Divine guidance in the form of a divine moral code. But in Hillary's liberal "village,"[83] you can kiss most of these *blessings* good-bye.

This is as good a place as any to delve deeper into Christian teaching about benevolence and "privilege." And one way we can approach this to examine it from the perspective of the contrast between **wants** (optional things) and **needs** (essential things).

America's decline is being assisted today by some of the teaching found in many churches. The suggestion in the next few paragraphs is that one of the current theological fads is at odds with biblical truth. Furthermore, these wrong-headed ideas are at best myopic. At their worst they are major contributors to societal disaster.

Taking care of our brother's **needs** is something that is right, or just. One teacher made the comment that there are over 2000 Bible references which compel believers to provide for each other. I can't count that high, but he's probably right. But it's more intrinsic than just scripture. If we have Christ living within us, there's just no way we can walk past the needy without offering help. The context for all our actions is Christ-like agape love.

So the Bible teaches us we should do whatever it takes to supply others' needs. But it says nothing in favor of supplying their wants. I realize that in some uses "wants" can be synonymous with "needs." I am emphatically drawing a contrast between these two terms here. Needs are what are necessary for sustenance. Wants are what are desired for optional personal pursuits. Needs = shelter, bread, water, clothing, etc. Wants = lobster, cell phones, smart phone, whatever, you name it. Needs are life's essential necessities. Wants are life's optional accessories.

Let's move on. One key concept in all this Bible teaching and in our efforts to emulate the person of Jesus is **justice**. Justice has to do with what is fair, with what is deserved. A simple biblical application of this principle is that my needy brother, simply by virtue of his humanity, deserves to have his needs met. Christians accept by faith that this principle is just, right. (A side question: In a non-Christian, relativistic world view, where does one get the imperative for agape love? Put another way, why is lack of compassion, or even hate, wrong? Better yet: If there's no right or wrong, how can progressives say anything is "wrong"?)

So the concept of justice emanates from God and means nothing if it does not compassionately act in a way seeking to assure that no other human being goes thru life needy. These actions are demanded by the fact that all of us are children of a benevolent Creator. We are a family. And we are, to some extent, our brother's keeper. To what extent are we thus? That is the question. And this question is further emphasized, not by asking "How little can I give?" but by asking "What did God, in his infinite wisdom, reveal to us about how to address the problem of needs?" Here's some of the biblical teaching we find. Some of these are addressed to the givers, and some to the recipients:

- Every man, even an enemy, is your neighbor.
- As we have the opportunity, let us do good to all men, especially believers.
- Do not oppress the fatherless, widows, and strangers.
- Do not pervert justice by favoring _either the poor or the rich_.
- Do not neglect the needy on the basis of race.
- Do not give entitlements to unqualified widows. (But do "enroll" those who meet certain qualifications)
- Food is not an entitlement of the able-bodied who refuse to work.
- Be content with food and clothing.
- Your heavenly Father knows your needs: Food, drink, and clothing. Do not worry about these.
- Be willing to work according to your ability, to provide for yourself with your own hands, and to earn things to share with others.

- Do not harvest every scrap of produce from the fields or vineyards. Leave the margins and the excess for the poor to reap. (Author's note: This involves effort on their part, thus preserving their dignity.)
- Recognize that what Job owned, what the vineyard owner owned, and what Ananias and Saphira owned was their stewardship. And for all intents and purposes in this life, the material things were their possessions. While in their hands, these possessions were theirs to do with according to what they determined. They didn't answer to other men for this, but to God.
- Special circumstances may dictate times when Christians huddle together and "have all things common." Contributions put into the "common" pool in are to be given voluntarily.
- When a collection is taken up for needy Christians, the givers are to "purpose in their hearts" what they will give.
- These last four truths, and maybe some of the others, work from a principle of personal ownership. In this we are not accountable to other men, but to God.
  (In other words, as far as our relationship with other men is concerned there is a God-recognized right to private property.)
- What is Caesar's belongs to Caesar.
- Masters (and employers?) must remember: A worker is worthy of his hire.
- Slaves (and employees?) must remember: Serve your master as if serving God.
- If you are an employee, and are asked to sign a union card......... draw your own conclusion.
- Permit me to state another obvious conclusion: The biblically defined, and therefore acceptable, bottom line for quality of life is: Food, Clothing, Shelter.

I'm afraid this next point is going to be even more unpopular. But I am compelled to submit that justice is nothing, and loses its God-given meaning, if it has a modifying word in front of it. Think of *diversity justice*, *sexual orientation justice*, or *climate justice*. Or think especially of the phrase that started a landslide collapse of a truly wonderful principle: *social justice*. Listen to three people who are a lot smarter than I am:

> *[Social justice] does not belong to the category of error but to that of nonsense, like the term "a moral stone."*[84]

> *.........the notion of "rights" is a mere term of entitlement, indicative of a claim for any possible desirable good, no matter how important or trivial, abstract or tangible, recent or ancient. It is merely an assertion of desire, and a declaration of intention to use the language of rights to acquire said desire. In fact, since the program of social justice inevitably involves claims for government provision of goods, paid for through the efforts of others, the term actually refers to an intention to use force to acquire one's desires. Not to earn desirable goods by rational thought and action, production and voluntary exchange, but to go in there and forcibly take goods from those who can supply them!*[85]

> *Either "social justice" has the same meaning as "justice" – or not. If so – why use the additional word "social?" We lose time; we destroy trees to obtain paper necessary to print this word. If not, if "social justice" means something different from "justice" – then "something different from justice" is by definition "injustice."*[86]

The utopian mirage of perfect equality is sometimes sought through "Egalitarianism", which is defined either as *seeking equality of opportunity* or *seeking equality of outcomes*. If used in the second sense, *equality of outcomes*, egalitarianism becomes a destructive injustice, damaging both the looter and the looted. In fact, guaranteeing equal outcomes is possibly the greatest injustice of all. Here are three reasons why.

- *Egalitarianism removes incentives for entrepreneurship.* Sometimes the motivation is greed, and other times it's nobler than that. Regardless of the reasons people have for pursuing their creative dream, countless millions benefit from the results. Example: I don't know the nobility factor in the motivation for whoever designed and built my dishwasher, but it's here and I can let it do the dishes. And because someone designed and someone built this dishwasher, I find I have more and more time to torment the public with books like this.

- *Egalitarianism compromises mankind's advancement toward excellence.* Example: It is myopic, and maybe idiotic, to "mainstream" mentally ill children into classrooms in ways that hold back other students. If a medical solution is going to be found for some of man's mental illnesses, we're going to have to cut the geniuses loose and let them run on ahead. This is, after all, the best way to serve those with problems. The solution will come that way, and it will come a whole lot sooner.

- *Egalitarianism destroys the dignity of the recipient.* A real serious problem arises when folks continually get what they don't deserve, because every gift is a reminder of their inferiority. This same principle applies to God's grace, to gifts we receive from individuals, and to institutionalized welfare programs which go too far by supplying a lot more than mere sustenance, clothing and shelter.

Time for another movie illustration. This one's from *Jeremiah Johnson*. One scene begins with Jeremiah and Del Gue riding along, carrying a lot of Indian scalps and pelts, and leading several captured ponies. They are suddenly surrounded by Flathead Indians, who turn out to be relatively peaceful. Del and Jeremiah are escorted back to the village, and into a tepee where they sit down for an awkward powwow. The chief, Two-tongues Le Beau, gestures toward Jeremiah and gestures toward the scalps, and then says something in his native tongue. Del Gue interprets:

**Del Gue**: *He says the scalps are fierce...and the horses are fleet.*

**Jeremiah:** *Take them. And the ponies. I have no further use for them*

**Del Gue:** #*%+*@ *fool, you may have cooked our brains! He brought us here to honor you and you want to give him a gift. If he cannot give you a better one, it'll be an insult. He'll have to kill you.* (Note to you bleeding hearts who are given to waxing nostalgic about "noble savages": Having white men's brains cooked is not symbolism.)

Now I don't know a lot about Indians. The powwow in the tepee may not be typical or accurate. But the scene in the movie is instructive. It highlights the problems people create when gifts are given and there's no appropriate avenue for reciprocation. Human relationships can be devastated because gifts often implicitly carry an assumption of dependence. And people are thus forced to make one of three choices: To either accept the gift with its implication of inferiority and servitude, or to accept the gift and then give a better gift, or to rebel against the insult by killing the gift-giver.

In Christianity, Jesus' life and substitutionary death are the ultimate gifts. There's obviously no better reciprocal gift. So in this case our choices are reduced to two: We either accept the gifts with the implications of lordship and servitude, or we reject them and thus take an active role in crucifying God's Son.

In the movie, Two-tongues chose to give Swan, his daughter, to Jeremiah, and everybody held their breath while Jeremiah almost rejected her. But Jeremiah's final forced answer allowed Two-tongues to maintain his own sovereignty. There was a hastily scheduled wedding and everybody was happy. Everybody except Jeremiah and his bride.

There is a third application -- a real-life one -- with profound implications for modern American culture. Can't you see it? Some of the people I work with pay out $50-70,000 a year in taxes. If their money was handled more efficiently, and directed toward solving problems rather than buying votes, these taxpaying benefactors would be more than happy to pay. So, because of the Federal Government's wasteful incompetence, we see a measure of discontent from the ones paying the taxes. (And if that's not paying their fair share, I don't know what is. Don't you think it odd that Democrats have never defined what constitutes "fair share?")

But the larger problem in this third application is not with the gift-givers, but the gift-receivers. There's far more discontent on the part of the recipients. They are the ones who burn cars, riot in the streets, occupy and trash public parks and generally show an all-around attitude of ingratitude for the hand out. The ingratitude is not surprising – they are human beings after all, facing a central human problem inherent in the following truth:

> Entitlements foster dependency -
> Dependency creates dependents –
> Dependents must accept the implication of inferiority (Or they must trash the gift-giver.)

We understand how the principle of dependency works to destroy natural order in the animal kingdom. Why is it so hard to understand and/or admit the human applications? After all, they don't feed bears, do they?[87]

Our government tries to muddy the water enough to promote the illusion that Washington is the benefactor

45

of those who are dependent. And for the non-literate the effort is successful.[88] But that's a smoke and mirrors charade and any one with open eyes and minimal intelligence can see Washington has no money of its own. All this was set in motion by FDR[89], accelerated by LBJ, and hyper-accelerated by Barry Sotero. Look out, my friend.....you're the gift giver, and you can't be allowed to live. The bear is about to tear up your camping trailer. Eventually the recipients will evolve into serial looters. And then they will be coming for you.

The bottom line is this: Efforts at entitlement aiming at equality of outcomes are arguably the greatest injustice of all. If we take from the wealthy to give to the poor mainly because a few effete intellectuals in the Harvard teachers' lounge have decided the wealth gap is too big, we will kill the God-given principle of true justice.

Remember this profound saying:

> *Injustice anywhere is a threat to justice everywhere.* (Dr.
> Martin Luther King)

Current application: When Eric Holder argues that "blowback" is justified, he is thus threatening justice everywhere. And he's being deliberately devious. Either that or he's ignorant or ill-informed or insane.

# 10 Court Coup d'état

A coup d'état is *a sudden decisive exercise of force in politics; especially: the violent overthrow or alteration of an existing government by a small group.*[90]

No need to be misleading here; we have only a 75% metaphor. What happened in the courts was not sudden. And it was only violent with respect to decency, morality and the lives of future generations. In other words, there's been no bloodshed except by terrorists like Bill Ayers and Bernadette Dorn. And what about all that blood spilled in the womb? Isn't that violence, too? (But we'll never really know for sure will we? All the first-hand witnesses have been liquidated.) Those exceptions notwithstanding, where this metaphor really shines is in saying "overthrow or alteration of an existing government by a small group."

An Indian parable goes like this: A thimbleful of water gets in a boulder's crack, seasons cycle, the water freezes, and the boulder splits.[91] Questions: How can activists fracture the rock-solid foundations of a decent, God-fearing country? Or, how can these activists get to practice their weird impulses and fringe fetishes free of guilt while destroying the American way of life? Answer: The courts.

The judicial coup is a story all by itself. How did this coup happen? First note that normalphobes had no respect for law. The decent people did, mainly because they had instructions in their User's Guides to "Honor the King." So, if you could get a judge to make a decision, the decent people were in the default mode to honor it. It became a goal of the agitators to select sympathetic judges in order to produce some unpopular, and even bizarre, interpretations of the laws. And then they could sit back and watch principled people struggle with what they should do. These bizarre law rulings are what a lot of people are talking about when they bring up judicial activism.

Here's another observation highlighting some of the factors involved in manipulation of the courts. It's significant to note that in the '60s and '70s anyone with 20/50 vision could tell just by the way people looked who was normal and who was normalphobic. The fringe people in the shallow part of the Bell curve all looked ............ well, fringy. Back then the way a person presented himself didn't matter in this one respect: All the key progressive issues had to be decided in the courts since there was no way people were going to vote, for example, to allow doctors to use tiny egg-beaters to scramble up unborn babies. And no way would they allow innocent toddlers to be fodder for sick cultural experiments that sentenced these children's' one chance at living to family life with same-sex parents. In cases like these, public opinion was obviously a lost cause. So it didn't much matter how the normalphobes looked, and they chose to look like slouches. In your face slouches. There was a 30-year period in there (ca. 1965-1995) where visual cues were accurate predictors for liberalism and conservatism.

Here are three examples of what is meant by visual cues:

> **1.** In the late '60s, if someone wore sandals and had long hair, there was Predictability Factor (PF) of 75% liberal. The PF went up 1% for each day a given person was willing to go without a shower. 2% for no shower + no shave.

> **2.** Any worldview influences a person's life choices, and those life choices are therefore ideological indicators with varying amounts of predictability. The exception to this rule is ethnicity and/or skin color. Neither of these is

48

by choice, but they are characterized by a high degree of predictability. Which brings us to #3..........

*3.* Skin Color – Since FDR an average of 90% of African Americans were (and still are) Democrats.[92] In the city I just left, Memphis, it's more like 98%. (Example #3 here is just a simple statement of fact.......why do people get mad at this?)

Now things are different in some key respects. The old rules for predictability are less true today than they were back then. One reason is deviancy has been defined so far downward that all the big liberal gains have been made. It's only left to clean up the margins. Another reason: The whole electorate has been dumbed down to the point where more than 50% can be easily fooled. It's actually possible for normalphobes to win public elections -- an outcome that should be impossible just by definition. So, ideological positions don't matter as much anymore. And *Image is everything.*

I almost forgot.........Here's one more PF indicator that's nearly 100% accurate: If you go to one of those rallies on the Washington Mall, and if you notice that most of the people there are carrying around pocket copies of the US constitution, you can be absolutely sure you're at a rally of the decent people. You're among conservatives.

Back to the idea of judicial activism.......remember Maud Wilson? We last saw her as one of 5 people at her daughter's softball game. (That's 5 counting the umpires.) The whole situation made Maud mad, so she set out to get revenge by emasculating collegiate athletic programs. Ultimately her legacy would be this: Just so softball players could feel as important as Heisman winners, schools wound up having to spend the same money on ribbon twirling as they do on football. The key element forcing this change was called "*Title 9.*"

Here are some quotes about *Title 9*:

> (*Title 9 involves*) *adopting a quota system for varsity sports participation, promising that women's share*

49

*would come out within 5 percentage points of female enrollment....*

*Female litigators make little secret of their animus toward football, many evidently agreeing with University of Wisconsin-Milwaukee professor Margaret Carlisle Duncan that it's "an institution that promotes male Dominance."*

*The premise of the gender-equity movement is simple: Women's sports should get just as much money, atten-tion, and participation as men's.*[93]

This legislation was mostly Maud Wilson's doing. But she went on to do a lot more damage. Her total contribution to humanity wound up being pervasive and destructive. It's a long story, but really interesting. Here goes.

After Maud got home from Woodstock, she got a Social Justice Law degree from Cal Berkeley. She minored in Religious Studies. That last accomplishment was amazing, 'cause in Berkeley you could get a four-year degree without ever opening a Bible.

Maud's degree was practically worthless, so she wandered aimlessly for several years. Her whole purpose in life seemed to be simply trying to live it up down at the head shops and trolling for liquor in the bars. It was just a moment of incredible luck, but one night she got drunk and wound up in the bed of a perfect stranger who turned out to be a US senator. Woodstock's influence was in full force here, so the affair had no moral implications for Maud. Problem was, it wasn't morally neutral for him. So she was able to do some *carpe diem* by blackmailing him for a federal judgeship. 9th circuit, California. Fast forward a few years and the aforementioned *Title 9* becomes law.

If you strip all the non-essentials away you'll find that *Title 9* is sim-ply a very expensive way to admit that females are physically weaker, and are in fact inferior, to men in a few specific areas of life. (Men, of course, are inferior in others.) Anyway, now we have the Federal Government demanding that the whole country validate a bunch of collegiate streamer twirlers who are still getting low scores from the Czechs.[94] If we don't control our gasping laughter, we're intolerant and guilty of hate-thought. A related modern absurdity is the fact that we've reached the point where one of the most important and overriding considerations is to not hurt anyone's feelings.

Maud's fame with the chattering class was further enhanced when she wrote the majority opinions for two judicial decisions. The first decision was called **Babies vs Roe-v-Wade.** It was released to the public at 3:58pm on a Friday. The second decision settled a suit brought before the court by her daughter. It was called **Erica Wilson vs. Roe-v-Wade**. It adjudicated a complaint seeking redress on behalf of an unborn person, and it was released one minute later at 3:59pm on that same day. What happened in that milli-fraction of man's history helps us quantify the extent of the progressives' insanity. It also says a lot about Maud's wisdom. We'll go through all the pertinent facts in both cases.

**Erica Wilson v. Roe-v-Wade:** Like her mother, Erica graduated from Cal, and since she wasn't an illegal alien, and only got a partial scholarship for softball, she had to do what she could to pay off her student loans. Her degrees were also worthless. Her major was in Climate Justice; her minor was in Diversity Conflict Resolution.

Erica had partnered up with the softball team's shortstop and they were living together across the Bay in the Castro district. These two played the bongos for loose change down on the Warf, collected welfare, and supplied their bongs by using food stamps when the other government programs fell short. But all this simply wasn't enough. They felt like the American Dream was a worthy goal, even though the idea of "America" was despicable to everyone connected in any way with Berkeley. So they came up with an entrepreneurial plan. And it was very lucrative. She and her partner figured out they could get $100,000 a pop for being artificially inseminated to become surrogate mothers for Bay area male couples who were dying to have children in their "families."

Erica was 7 months into her second $100,000 pregnancy when she hit a bump in the road. Literally. She had always been conflicted about the damage all the SUVs were doing to the sacred environment. So she did her part by making the "moral" choice to drive a Nissan Leaf. She was part of BCC -- the Berkley Conservation Co-op. This socialist group had a fleet of 500 of cute little cars that they communally shared. The cars were easy to spot since they were painted a bright, in-your-face, lime green.

It was time for Erica's third trimester check-up back across the Bay at Cal Med. The wind was really blowing this day. And there was a pothole right in the middle of the exit ramp. Her Leaf hit the pothole, bounced up a few inches, and then was blown clean off the ramp. Gaia[95] must've been watching over Erica, 'cause she landed up-side down in a half-full recycle dumpster. Eyewitness accounts were vague because of all the other leaves swirling all around. Many witnesses actually did see the Leaf in the dumpster, but they thought it was regular household garbage.

The plastic in the dumpster cushioned the impact a lot; so much so that there wasn't much of a noise.

The air bags did their job and inflated. Erica escaped with hardly a scratch to her body. Until she unbuckled her seatbelt and fell to the ceiling of the car. That's when the seat belt caught on three of her facial rings and ripped them right out.

Sadly, Erica's body wasn't the only one involved in the crash. Her baby didn't survive.

Five seconds after impact the Cal football team bus passed by on its way to the big game at Palo Alto. One minute later a Catholic priest across the street at Starbucks got thru to 911. Ten minutes later the EMT's arrived. One hour later Erica was sitting up in the hospital bed recovering. One day later she was back home in the city. One week later she was in the offices of the Randall H. Scott law firm plotting the mother of all lawsuits.

It was a legal dilemma. If the fetus was just simple, replaceable tissue, then there was no reason to make such a big case. But if the fetus was, in fact, a person, then the financial implications would be enormous. So Erica, along with her team of attorneys, decided to plead the case on behalf of the unborn person, alleging that several entities had intruded on the baby's "fetal privacy" by contributing to an invasion of the safety and sanctity of the womb. You can see how tricky this is getting. I mean the only thing standing in the way of their efforts was the 1973 Supreme Court ruling **Roe v Wade**, which ruled in favor of a woman's right to privacy, while implicitly denying that an unborn baby had a right to privacy. Now this was California, mind you, and no news outlet would dare publish the name of the case as **The Personhood of Erica's baby vs Roe v Wade**. So the lawyers went into the stealth mode and called it **Erica Wilson vs Roe v Wade.** They were hoping to keep it on the hush-hush so Fox News would be in the dark until after the final verdict.

The lawsuit sought damages of $500,000,000.00 with the potential of judge stipulated triple damages. Named in the lawsuit were Nissan, the airbag makers, the Cal football team, Catholic priests, and Starbucks.

> **Nissan:** Nissan was alleged negligent because they failed to place flashing warning lights in the Leaf's instrument panel that should've said
>
> > **Warning**: Do Not Operate Vehicle in Winds Greater Than 18 MPH! Do Not Operate on Roads Designed for Full-Size Vehicles!
>
> **Airbag Makers:** The airbag was also missing a warning.....
>
> > **Warning:** Deployment may cause regurgitation, possibly even miscarriage.
>
> **Cal Football Team:** The football team went right by the crash, but 70 out of 70 of the team members were looking at the cheerleader bus in the next lane. In situations

like this, facts don't matter much to wrongful injury lawyers, and the Golden Bears were charged with leaving the scene. But the real reason they were named was because the football team was the only manly thing left in Berkley, and somehow their manliness makes some women remember that in the past they had to be the ones to clean dishes and have babies. Doesn't make any sense I know, but there it is.

**The Catholic Priest:** Erica had wanted to terminate her 2nd pregnancy early on, and was within an inch of signing the paperwork at Planned Parenthood. But she gave in to a vague twang of guilt. After the accident she was in the hospital bed and had a chance to reflect. Then she realized that the only way she could've had a conscience would've been from left over residual brain waves created the one time she visited mass with her best friend in the 3rd grade. Where else could she have developed a conscience? Certainly not from Maud. So the priest was sued for mental cruelty.

**Starbucks?** It was their rented dumpster.

The case was denied in two lower courts on the grounds of being............. ridiculous. But it advanced on appeal, and was finally placed on the 9th Circuit docket. We don't know the name of the secretary in the office that day. She has to live her life "in the closet" because she's one of a dozen pro-life Christians still left in the state of California. But she was the one who read the brief. And then she called James Dobson.

Enter the second case: ***Babies vs. Roe v Wade***. The secretary's phone call to Family Talk was like an alarm going off for the decent people, because they realized Erica's lawyers were arguing that the unborn had a right to privacy. Family Talk's pro-life motto was "Be the Voice for Those Who Have No Voice" -- No, wait....that's actually the motto for the World Wildlife Fund. No, wait......the WWF actually got that from Proverbs 31:8.

Anyway, the pro-lifers were the only ones in the whole world looking for opportunities to stand up for the truly voiceless and utterly defenseless. They thought that bringing both cases up before the 9th Circuit at the same time would be instructive. Both their thinking and their case were airtight and simple: If Erica's unborn baby had a right to privacy, then all babies have a right to privacy.

Both cases came before the 9th circuit court in the same session. Maud ruled opposite ways in her decisions. She solved the dilemma by ruling against Family Talk *first*. Since it was *first*, she could keep a straight face while saying there was no precedent. And she then ruled in favor of Erica by reasoning that "Social Justice" outweighs the need to determine when life actually begins. It may be clarifying to think of that last decision as ordering reparations for the Gay, Lesbian, Transgender, Gender Neutral, and Electric Car communities.

Maud awarded triple damages. But she said there would be no monetary obligation from UC Berkley as long as they agreed to totally dismantle their men's athletic program.

Maude made the covers of *Time* and *Newsweek* again, and this time she was heralded as a modern day Solomon. And she *was* like Solomon, but only if you can forget the has-nothing-to-do-with-anything fact that Solomon saved the baby.[96] After all that build up, the court decision sure seems anti-climactic, doesn't it? But this is the way the world ends, not with a bang, but a whimper.[97] I don't know what else to say about this except that principles aren't a big deal with the Frisbee crowd.

(Now I know that story was long-winded. Apologies here for diverting you attention for so long. I'd advise checking the White House records to see if Obama passed any more destructive unconstitutional executive orders while you were busy reading this.)

You may have noticed the odd timing of the release of these two 9th Circuit decisions. They came within one minute of each other right before closing late on a Friday. This is instructive in that it highlights a favored tactic of the progressives. They typically try to announce any momentous decision between close of business Friday and mid-night Saturday.[98] Why? Several reasons: Saturday is a slow news day. And all the decent people are off watching baseball or NASCAR any-way. Of course we all know where those same decent people are on Sunday. They're holed up in a stained-glass sanctuary, bitterly clinging to God. So Saturday and Sunday present the left with a great opportu-nity to pass out unchallenged propaganda on Face the Nation, etc. By the time Monday night's news cycle rolls around, all the Liberal spin is already written up as fact on Wikipedia. By then it's old news.)

Maud also always ruled in favor of the ACLU. This is a special Frisbee club whose sole purpose is to destroy Western Culture by protecting the guilty. Just think about what life was like before ACLU: No locks, no security systems, no chain-link barbed wire fences around schools, school discipline that worked, no personal injury lawyers, real short death-rows, etc. Now it's the innocent citizens who are going through the death-throes.

Of course there was always the threat of not getting it right back then and punishing a non-criminal. And it's certainly a worthy pursuit to try to protect the innocent. But the net effect of ACLU efforts is turning out to be protection of the guilty. How many "non-criminals" (law-abiding citizens) are paying the penalties now? Just think how many more innocent citizens have been harmed or killed because of the ACLU's agitation litigation. I would guess crime is ten times more likely today as a direct result of legal maneuvers purportedly trying to protect the innocent. What's your guess? The practical result is that we've lost a lot more of the good, and protected a lot more of the bad. What does the User's Guide say?

> *Because justice is not speedily executed, so the hearts*
> *of men are set to do evil.*[99]

The sinister fruits of the ACLU torment us in countless subtle ways. Just one here for the record: Next time you come home from buying the groceries and try to get in the car to unload them from the passenger side, you'll probably discover the door is still locked because you didn't push the remote twice to unlock all the doors. Won't you join me in cursing a pathetic legacy? Take a deep breath and then fill in your own blank: _____ ACLU!

And another thing, before ACLU, companies didn't have to spend billions of $$$ on "sensitivity training." Sure, if someone is abusive they should be counseled or even fired. But if someone just "feels" abused, then it's only pseudo-abuse and the wimps just need to grow up.

One example of pseudo-abuse: A co-worker of mine was sentenced to 6 weeks of sensitivity training after a minority walked by his office and overheard a particular radio show.

Another example: The Liberals cried "foul" and threw dust in the air all because Rick Lazio violated Hillary Clinton's "space" in the New York Senate debates.[100] OH MY! Lazio walked toward her with a piece of paper!!!! And he VIOLATED HER SPACE!!!! It's reminiscent of the 5 and 7 year olds in the back seat of the car. They've just been separated because the bumping was getting too rough. What happens next? "He's *looking* at me mean." Similar event, except the children don't consciously choose to act immature.

It's just a random, semi-related thought at this point, but has anyone else noticed that when the Frisbee-throwers go to court their main argument necessarily implies that they're saying "I'm weak! I'm weak!" What's up with that? Ever hear of a normal person doing that?

Maud was instrumental in creating a special group of crimes called "hate-crimes". There was a rumor running around that she was preparing to rule that hate-*thought* is a crime. You know "Cop's face is filled with hate"[101] -- stuff like that.

But Maud didn't get to make that ruling. And our cover girl never made it to the Supreme Court. Here's what happened: In order to not hurt anyone's feelings -- in order to "enfranchise" everyone -- the Supreme Court began to look more and more like the Star Wars Bar scene. The politically correct justice system corrupted itself faster that Maud could corrupt herself, and relatively speaking she became too "normal." Barack Hussein Obama skipped over our *Title 9* heroine and appointed a 16 year-old transsexual because he/she was the only one who could implement *"If it feels good - do it!"* on behalf of children and transsexuals. The country got a two-fer, maybe even a three-fer, on that one. You bet. And in about 33 minutes of more reading you're going to learn how Obama could have even worse plans for the Star Wars Bar.

That summarizes the whole of Maud judicial career – but she wasn't done yet. She retired from the bench to become a leading activist for Planned Parenthood. She lost her last ounce of humanity by supporting partial birth abortion. She, and all the other inhumans, never realized that if the abortion question was above the President's pay grade,[102] then no one could say it was *right*. In other words, if you don't know when life begins, then you don't when life ends. And if you don't know when life ends, then you don't know whether or not you've ended life. It's a shot in the dark. And here's a related news flash: Man is not God. Now just pause for a prayerful, agonizing moment and look at our carnage: *1,600,000 per year in America -- Land of the Free and Home of the Brave. 50 million since Roe v. Wade. And all this because some woman, somewhere, sometime might possibly get pregnant from rape or incest.* This is absolute inhuman madness.

# 11  Firing from the Mosque

Have you begun to notice something odious in the way these Frisbee throwers operate?  It's right there in front of you when you read things like "she had a morally-neutral affair with a US Senator and blackmailed him........" The problem is this: Having even a hint of moral guidance is an expensive virtue because it can be a fatal burden in any argument with godless scoundrels.  (Remember that the idea of moral account-ability was way too inconvenient for the mud-wrestlers back in August, 1969, so it had to go.)

Another way to look at this: People on both sides of the ideological divide behave badly. But pause just a second. Think with me. And then accept or reject this proposition: *No moral code = No hypocrisy*. Only one side has hypocrites.  There is no "double standard" because only one side has standards.  When have you ever heard anyone accuse a progressive of hypocrisy?  The point is there can be no reasonable dis-course, because one side uses the moral aspirations of their opponents as a tool to destroy their credibility. That's not so much trying to win an argument as it is trying to destroy the very basis of goodness.

It may be helpful to understanding the point here by examining terror-ists' behavior.  These sub-human life forms will take babies hostage at knife point.  Or join up with Hamas to fire rockets aimlessly into Israel, hoping to hit the jackpot and blow up a kindergarten or a hospital. Think

59

of it as *Firing from the Mosque.* One side is working to protect the innocent. The other side is working to destroy innocence. Example: Maybe they'll go get a dull knife and slowly saw off the head of a random living person[103] who was just trying to help them rebuild their country. There's only one story here. Unless the spineless media are willing to report that one side has lost its humanity and lost its right to exist, then there's nothing to report.

Here at home in the political arena we're not dealing with overt terrorism. And while it's not as dramatic as a televised beheading, the principle remains the same. This is how decent people like Trent Lott[104] and George Allen[105] are hounded right out of the arena of ideas. First, they make some weak, obscure jokes. Then they have to answer to their own lofty standards. And then all the feigned nausea and "righteous" indignation -- all the chatter -- make it impossible for observers to remember it was Lott's and Allen's striving for decency that was their weakness. There's a real potential for a lot of collateral damage when a principled person challenges the ideology of someone with no principles.

There is a scene in the first Narnia movie with chilling implications for where we are today in our society; for where we've been since the slime event at Woodstock. The boy Edmund has sold himself to the White Witch, Jadis, for a handful of sweets. Aslan the Lion is Narnia's exiled ruler. He has forgiven the sorrowful, repentant boy. Now Jadis has an audience with Aslan, and she's demanding Edmund's life. The Lion says he has forgiven the boy. Jadis tries to turn one of the lion's strengths into a weakness. She points out, with a sarcastic sneer, that since Aslan is all about being absolutely, purely just, Edmund cannot be simply "forgiven." Points out that the price for transgression will have to be paid. She says *"Aslan knows that unless I have blood as the Law says, all Narnia will be overturned and perish in fire and blood."* Aslan responds: *"I was there when the law was written."* Aslan then arranges the only possible transaction with Jadis that will atone for the boy's wrong. We'll leave for another book the meaning behind this "atonement," but here's a hint: It is really, really, really good news. Each one of us has been seduced by forbidden sweets. We have all succumbed.

There is none righteous, not one. All sin. All fall short. We are in a horrible dilemma. But now, for everyone willing to listen, the news of the atonement is the best news we'll ever hear. I earnestly pray that I have piqued your interest.

Narnia's implication for what is proposed in this chapter of our book is obvious, isn't it? Jadis may as well be saying "You try to be noble, so you can't fire at me – not while I'm hiding in this Mosque." Or, "I'm in here among the civilians, go ahead and kill us." Or, "'Macaca'? None of us knows what that means, but you can't say it anyway 'cause you say you're all about decency." Or even, "You believe in the constitution, so sit there and act like you enjoy it when I burn this flag." People today, like Jadis, are using what is good and decent in society to destroy the good and the decent.

Progressive leftist aren't saddled with the inconvenience of moral constraint. Ted Kennedy gets off scott-free after pushing womanizing and drunkenness completely off the bridge. Bill Clinton stains the Oval Office and is still revered. Barney Frank hangs around even after his child porn and drug convicted male "partner" runs a prostitution ring out of Frank's house. And drug-dealing Marion Barry gets re-elected. The list could go on endlessly, or at least until the printer runs out of ink. Is it any surprise that about 100% of convicted criminals are Democrats? Or 100% (margin of error +/-2%) of Gays? Or 100% (+/-0%) of Larry Flynt? It's only on the left that people don't have to answer to a moral code. How convenient that they've made their cowardly pragmatic transition to "Values."

As emphasis, it's probably useful at this point to do some more polarization and clarify our terms. Clarification is utterly simple: the "Decent People" are those voluntarily attempting to hold themselves accountable to standards of decency. Is it too much to ask that everyone remember this is more about their lofty aspirations, than it is about their lowly performance?

We can also clarify our terms by approaching the subject negatively. In other words, by showing what is not decent. That's utterly simple, too. The photograph of Obama's buddy, Bill Ayers, standing on the American flag says it all. A picture is truly worth a thousand words. *And he's proud of this.* Just ask him.

Here's more negative definition. This time in the form of hopeless audacity. Take a look at Barack Obama. In the picture below he's gesturing while commenting about John McCain's campaign. This picture was taken from a clip still running on YouTube. If you can find the recording made by ABC, watch that one and pay close attention to the crowd. When his middle finger goes out, the crowd cheers. There are two women sitting in the back row who are captured in the clip. One is wearing black and the other white. The lady in white leans over to the one in black and says "What did he just do?" The lady in black responds: "He just flipped him off." The lady in white then laughs in delight. It's easy to read their lips. A lot of people try to cover for Obama on this one. He is after all so

genuinely classy and innocent. Just look at the crease in his pants.[106] But, let's not be naïve here........ let's let the ones who were actually there tell us what they thought.

As long as the decent people at least try to

hold to their ideals, they can't really lose in ideological confrontations. Not personally, anyway. But what *is* lost is another incremental measure of the common good. It should be enough consolation that the decent folk have held on to their humanity while their antagonists have lost theirs. It would be enough, except that our children and grandchildren are left defenseless before the overwhelming moral carnage.

# 12  The Death of Meaning

If you haven't guessed by know, let me make it clear: This rant is a cry (maybe it's just a whimper) against the obvious causes of the disintegration of our God-blessed America.  And one great fear is that we're all going to wake up one day to find there's No Meaning.  The case will be made here again, this time in chronological order.  Well, I take that back.  It starts out chronological, but then gets aimless.  Anyway, think of this as a kind of ABC's or maybe even Cliff's Notes for the rise and fall of America.  3 things going up, 1 pivotal event, then 21 going down.  After a great run up, the last 60 years have been mostly a downward spiral – much  like a commode flush.  Counter-clockwise in the Northern Hemisphere.  I tell you this, hoping that every time you flush for the rest of your life you will think of progressive Liberalism.  But it's actually much worse than it sounds, because here in the cultural arena the refuse refuses to go away.

## 25 KEY EVENTS IN THE RISE AND FALL OF AMERICA

## PRE-FLUSH-------------------------------------------------------------

> *A* *is for* *A*nthem.  *1814.*  Written by Francis Scott Key.
> Chest-thumping national pride.

*B* is for *B*aseball. *1845.* Invented by Andrew Doubleday. (Curve ball alert: it was actually Alexander Cartwright)

*C* is for '*C*omplishment. *1869 thru 1969.* America, now the peak embodiment of Western Civilization and unhindered by social-ism, was on a roll. Americans had only 2% of the world's popu-lation but they produced 95% of the world's advancements thru the mid-20th century. (Don't really know if that last statement is true or not, but I *feel* it -- see the letter *P*.) We did this while con-suming less than 15% per anum of the world's natural resources. Probably the best stewardship the Earth could've hoped for. There was Electricity, the Cotton Gin, the Steam engine, Light Bulbs, Telephone, Radio, Television, Locomotive, Automobile, Airplane, Computer, Cross the Atlantic, Break the Sound Barrier, Land on the Moon. And win the Big War, win the Bigger War, stop the Communists. Emancipate the slaves, elevate the women.

Overall, the gains Americans provided for humanity have been tre-mendous. Nothing like it in the annals of civilization. We did this in the span of only around 100 years. That's something like 1.6667% of recorded history. For all of my adult life, I've been proud.

# FLUSH------------------------------------------------------------

*D* is for *D*etestable, *D*espicable, *D*ung. *1948-1953:* Communism showed up in Hollywood, the army, and government. Raw sew-age was beginning to run in the streets. Richard Nixon, Joseph McCarthy, and other Congressmen tried to clean up the mess. Their efforts stirred up a beehive. A swarm of Leftist activists got real mad.

# POST-FLUSH---------------------------------------------------

*D* is also for *SDS,* 1962. The McCarthy flush didn't work. The refuse refused to go away. The activists, along with their children and comrades inherited the grudge from the first **D**. They simmered, stewed and whined for about 7 years, then huddled and formed the Students for Democratic Society (1960). Two years later they all got together at PortHuronMichigan to make a "Statement." It was issued at dawn on *June 15th, 1962,* as sort of a "Dream of a Vision." Happy little peace and love thoughts all around. They thought the sun was rising on a brave new world. You could just *feel* the impending Age of Aquarius. We'll have to give Tom Hayden[107] a pass on that one, 'cause drugged-out perceptions can be a bit foggy. I'll bet he wasn't even facing East. Bet nobody brought a compass. Bet nobody even knew what a compass was. No Boy Scouts, or engineers, or scientists in this group.

**E** is for **E**nvironmentalism. Also *1962*. Rachel Carlson wrote Silent Spring. Planted some seeds that flowered so beautifully and fragrantly into the Sierra Clubbers. Don't know what to think, though, 'cause someone else told me their seeds just grow weed.

Carlson's book also led to banning DDT. But that's OK, we don't miss it today. And about 20 million dead African children[108] don't miss it either. You know; out of sight, out of mind

**F** is for **F**risbee. *1964*. One of the PortHuronMichigan activists went home, ate a pizza, and then discovered that a spinning pizza plate will hold a controlled trajectory from the living room all the way back into the kitchen. So he worked with the capitalist system to get a patent.[109] Called his pizza plate the *Frisbee*. The Frisbee was the fulcrum which enabled societal leverage for the emerging normalphobic life-form. It was the opposite, mirror-image, of what baseball was for the normal folks.

**G** is for **G**reat Society. Also *1964*. President Lyndon Johnson invented his own Frisbee. Called it *The Great Society*. From our hindsight perspective we can see his Frisbee's trajectory. Always downward. And when loaded up with a bunch of cash and entitlements it goes almost straight down. The more we pile on it, the faster it goes. Wonder what ole LBJ would think about it now?

*H & I are for* **H***oly* **I***llusions, Batman!* Goes without saying (or does it?) that when terminology is accurate it gets in the way of those who want to change things from the current state to a reformer's desired state. Controlling the terminology is how the current crop of agitators work around the margins and in the shadows to advance a nefarious agenda.

In an effort to promote decency, regular folks developed some clear, simple, obvious rules. Like "Don't blow up the Pentagon" and "Don't burn down the ROTC building" and "Don't snuff out defenseless human life in the womb." When these rules got in the way of the agitators, they got a new set of "rules" by introducing new terminology. Example: They needed to break the law in order to make the law-abiding people jump through some hoops, so the Frisbee throwers' indecent "crimes" became "civil disobedience."[110]

And if they wanted to do something that made no-sense-what-soever it became "politically correct." Then "politically correct-ness" -- PC -- got a life of its own and took over the language. It was like turning on an airplane's autopilot.

"Riots" became "Peace Marches"
"Abortion" became "Choice"
"Abnormal" became "Normal"
"Morals" became "Values"
"Terrorism" became "Man-caused Disasters"
"Terrorists" became "Victims of American Arrogance"
"Wars" became "Overseas Contingency Operations"
"Trashing Public Sanctuaries" became "Occupy Movements"
"Racial Hatred Toward Whites" became "Justified Blowback"

"Climate Change" became "Global Cooling"
   became "Global Warming"
   became "Climate Change"

(And "DarylHannah" became a "Science Advisor."
And that's how we got a "consensus")

This brings us to what may be the most breathtaking manipulation of all. It has been mentioned before, but saved here in this list for last. This example involves a shamelessly obscene co-opting of one of God's gracious gifts: *Justice.*[111]

"Inefficient Government Redistribution of Forcibly Confiscated Wealth" became "Social Justice"

(In other words, "Injustice" became "Social Justice")

"Pagan Earth Worship" became "Climate Justice"[112]
"Unbridled Sexual Promiscuity" became "Reproductive Justice"
"Anything you want to do" became "(Couple any word with) Justice"

We could continue on into the night with this pathetic business of coupling any word with justice, but that would wind up being *ad nauseum justice.* I hope you get the point. The more ridiculous the ideology, the more necessary the redefinition.

.
People need to wake up to this process that seeks to rewrite language in an effort to support the illusion of harmlessness. Just think about the gut reaction to the old terminology: "sodomy." There's a tremendous gulf between the impact of that word and phrases like "same-sex relations." So now the brakes are all the way off. And since morality died in the mud at Yasgur's farm, we can expect any imaginable absurdity. Like this one:

"Bestiality" becomes "Puppy Love"

69

Now, mind you, there are constraints inherent in PC. But the PC constraints work to prevent people from saying much of what is meaningful, decent, or accurate. For some unknown reason these constraints relaxed a bit during the 2010 political campaign. It was like someone flipped the autopilot switch to "off." That was when the term "Man Up" slipped into the discourse and was used by everybody who was anybody for about two weeks.[113]

The ACLU thought the use of "Man up" was overtly sexist, and began preparing legal action hoping to force over 90% of the Republicans into remedial behavior sessions, commonly called "sensitivity counseling." But then their research uncovered something called the "Man Up Campaign."[114] This initiative was being promoted by the United Nations, the Clintons, and even Barack Hussein Obama. So they dropped the lawsuit like a hot Dan Quayle potatoe.[115]

It would be perversely entertaining (if it wasn't so sad) to watch as people squirm while trying to come up with suitable solutions for some of their remaining language conundrums. The most glaring dilemma may be the progressives' crying need to come up with a gender-neutral personal pronoun. If you want more unintentionally humorous commentary about this, visit Wikipedia. It's no wonder the *Doctor-who-am-I?* counseling sessions are all filling up.

*J* is for Bon *Jour.* It's the greeting you'll probably get as you wander up to the Arc du Triomph in Paris. Take a moment to peruse this massive structure and let its meaning soak in. It's a commissioned celebration of France's conquest of other sovereign countries. Imperialism at its best (worst).

If the significance of that encounter escapes you, try something else for punctuation: Walk away from the Arc du Triomph down the Champs-Elysees for one kilometer. Turn right on Avenue

W. Churchill. Go one more kilometer, pay 9 euros and enter the rotunda on the south end of the Les Invalides building. There before you will be the remains of that despicable Bonaparte, sealed in 6 nested coffins of soft iron, mahogany, two of lead, ebony, and oak, all covered in an outer sarcophagus of red porphyry. His resting place is under an extravagant, massive dome. His coffin is the sole object in a room nearly large enough to house a D2 college basketball game. And there he lies in perpetually in state, like a world class hero.

Now think about this: Where in the US can you find such monuments? You won't find them in San Diego, Carmen.[116] Nor will you in any other American city. The United States could've owned The Philippines, Japan, Italy, Germany, Iraq, the Moon ("We came in peace for *all mankind*."[117]), and just about every Pacific Island between California and Hong Kong. How dare the French lecture us about imperialism? How dare anybody lecture us about imperialism? The only imperialism the US has ever engaged in is the effort to bring self-rule and true democracy to all people everywhere.

You'd think the simplest intellects would get it, but oh no, no way. Here comes a cheap shot from the cheap seats: An acquaintance, a (really) privileged 22 year-old son-of-a-doctor in my church, feels the need to make the following ignorant Facebook comment on July 4th, 2010:

> *Today, like all other days, we protest American Imperialism by declaring it just another day. Peace.*

It's pitiful that so many are burdened with so much perceived guilt for the way God has blessed them. And another thing -- wait just a minute. The structure of that young man's phrase sounds way too familiar.........that's it!.........He's trying to get Dan Rather's old job!

Hearing the young talk like this is depressing. For a while there we all had a glimmer of hope that the chattering class would all die out with Hillary.

*Alternately, J is for John Lennon.* This talented and wildly popular writer/performer seemed to always be consumed with protesting something or smoking something. In the late sixties he was fooled into becoming the front-man puppet of the left. Some of his songs became anthems for impossible utopian ideologies. *Imagine that.* And when you're done with that theme, imagine there's no meaning; you hardly have to try.

But late in life Lennon saw the error of his way, repented and embraced conservatism.[118] He even came to admire Ronald Reagan. The word got out and now Yoko is fit to be tied.

*K, L & M are for MLK. 1968.* He freed a lot of people, but it seems the good die young.[119] But, Martin Luther King, Jr. wasn't perfect. He compromised once just a little bit by suggesting that getting a degree "by mail" was just as good as getting it "by Yale." Who was he kidding?

The progressives exploited King's opening, consulted with Darwin and Sanger, and began whittling away at the dignity of a whole race of human beings. First, there was Integration, which was a good idea. And then there was Busing, which could've been good, but wasn't. But those two things weren't enough for the social engineers. Soon there was Day Care, then Welfare Moms, then Head Start, then Subjective Grading, then No Grading, then Cheat on the Grading, then Social Promotions, then Affirmative Action, then Hiring Quotas. Predictably, what followed was art graffiti, then music graffiti, then Presidential graffiti. And all kinds of crime: guns and pimps and drugs. Hoods and gangs. And a cohesive common element in all these cultural slides: Community Organizers.

So blacks began to be treated as an inferior human species. Progressivism permitted them to have lower standards for academic success and for decency. Example: obscene rap song lyrics – I don't know if it's still a marked contrast, but for a while about ten years ago you could switch back and forth between BET and MTV and get a feel for the obvious disparity.

Another example of disparate standards:

During George W. Bush's campaign we heard: "**OH NO! OH NO! HE DRANK A LOT OF BEER!**"

During Barry Sotero's campaign: "While excelling in college, Obama used some very serious drugs and even went so far that ...................... .  .  ."    (Hey! What happened to the volume on my  remote?????)

The effects of the disparity in the way different groups have been treated has proven cumulative and devastating. Any God-fearing human knows Blacks are better than this. _All men_ were _created_ – **CREATED!** -- equal. Everybody knows this unless they're snuggling up to Darwin and Margaret Sanger.[120] It's now quite obvious that the social policies of the past 50 years have given us a different kind of slavery with an even worse bottom line -- no dignity.  _Why do these people continue to be 90% Democrats?_

Alternately, **M** is for **M**exicans. They're being enslaved in a similar way. i.e., "Yes, you can come into our country. No, you don't have to bother with those silly standards all the other, more civilized, people have to meet. Here, just take these: This first piece of paper is your Social Security card, and that other one's a voter registration. Now get on along. We'll see you later in the truck, or on the farm, or in the voting booth."

There's another lesson for us to learn at this point from baseball. The effort to change society would've been better served to mirror sports in general and baseball in particular. In 1947 Jackie Robinson became the first black to play major league baseball. Robinson didn't say "My people have been left out of this for so long....we're so far behind.....we need shortened base paths, a closer fence, and 4 strikes. And while you're at it, limit the pitchers to 75 mph and no curve balls." No, he just quietly went about the business of proving himself. His accomplishments are a source of untarnished pride: 1949 National League MVP, Hall of Fame, 10 years as an all-star. Way to go, Jackie.

Now do the dyslexic shift from 1947 to 1974: Just a few years later and Henry Aaron stood at the plate in Atlanta Georgia, staring at the seeming impossible Babe Ruth home-run record. Twenty-seven short years, and black Americans arrived at this threshold without cutting any corners. As in every other sport, their dignity and pride were intact, even enhanced. It was April 8, 1974, and I (1 each / Southern white boy), along with my wife (1 each / Southern white girl) were cheering at the top of our lungs in a hotel in Gulfport, Mississippi. Vin Scully was calling the game:

> *What a marvelous moment for baseball; what a marvelous moment for Atlanta and the state of Georgia; what a marvelous moment for the country and the world. A black man is getting a standing ovation in the Deep South for breaking a record of an all-time baseball idol.*

## *N is for Needs -- And Needs are not Wants!*

*How freaking loud does this have to be said?*

Let's all take a deep breath and re-acquaint ourselves with the definitions of "needs" and "wants". This is basic, first-grade stuff. We've kind of lost our way, what with all the trillions of dollars flying out of the US Treasury.

> **Needs** = What is necessary to *sustain* life
> **Wants** = What is necessary to *enhance* life.

Therefore:

> **Needs** =  Food, shelter, clothing, and probably basic medical care.
> **Wants** = Fill in the blank _____
> with anything else.  (Hint: Includes cars, air-conditioning, video games, Nike shoes, home ownership, home mortgage, abortions, cell phones, you name it.)

Christian principles weigh in here.  Christianity is emphatic about taking care of the needy.  Christianity is also emphatic about refusing to care for the *un*-needy.  There's a theory clamoring for our attention here:

> Provide for the **needs** = preserve personal dignity.
> Provide for the **wants** = destroy personal dignity.

I submit that FDR's[121] and LBJ's[122] grand social experiments have proved something.  They've proved there's a direct causal correlation between providing for a person's wants and their loss of dignity.

But the real problems still remain unsolved.  We do need to do something about unmet needs.  And practically speaking, how hard could it be?  Just set up a couple thousand cots in a warehouse downtown, open up a soup & bread line, and advertise that anyone can stay there as long as they want, no names taken; no questions asked.  Provide clothes and basic medical care.  Hey, that set up would be way better than what the soldiers are getting on the battlefield.  Dignity will be preserved, while those who want more out of life will be motivated to get out ASAP. And the soon-to-be-infamous 10-year AGBM Study shows the reduction in national budget outlays will be somewhere north of 82%.[123]

We're a long way from solving just needs, and the entitlement class is about the same distance away from self-respect and dignity. Black males in particular need to man up - to own up to their courageous statement "I Am A Man." They need to quit listening to Al Sharpton and Jesse Jackson and Jeremiah Wright. They need to start listening (again) to Martin Luther King. They need to remember Jackie Robinson and Henry Aaron. Here's the challenge for all disadvantaged minorities: You've gotten more than enough laws to right all the wrongs. Now go out and show the world what you're made of.

*O* is for *O*bama.

> *1960. Or 1961, or 1962, or 1963* -- Sometime.
> Hawaii, or Kenya, or Malaysia -- Somewhere.
> Barry or Sotero or Soebarkah or Barack Hussein -- Whatever.
> Similarly, *O* is for Zer*O*.

*P* is for *P*ostmodernism. *1979.* Some Frenchman in leotards named Jean-Francois gave a kind of smoke-and-mirrors legitimacy to this latest fad in philosophy. No one really knows what postmodernism is since the old everything is the new nothing. But it's safe to say that it's now reasonable to be unreasonable. Actually, it's safe to say anything. (With this kind of accepted intellectual standards, this book can claim to be above criticism.)

*1984.* Jean-Francois Lyotard's' work, The Post Modern Condition, was translated into English. Then a lot of the religious under grads and grads went "WOW!" and began trying to force the Gospel into a postmodern wineskin. But we need to stop and ask ourselves something here: Is postmodernism really the way people are thinking? Or is it the way some self-proclaimed thinkers *think* we're thinking? Or, worse still, is it the way some disillusioned atheists *want* us to think? And, is postmodernism their idea of progress? It's instructive at this point to be reminded how a lot of people went gaga over nonsense from people like Freud, Marx, Kinsey, and L. Ron Hubbard. With our hindsight, we could arguably group all of them in with HomerSimpson. Postmodernism could be another one of these very expensive dead-ends.

We've already covered how ideas like *No-such-thing-as-morality* and *No-such-thing-as-God* found a foothold in the radical, protest '60s. Today we're helplessly watching these incomplete sentences flower into maturity by ushering in the era of *No-such-thing-as-meaning*. The new context (fertilizer, it turns out) is postmodernism. It seems impossible to turn this thing around -- there's way too much inertia. Pray to Heaven, or pay to Hell.

*P is also for Plastic* **SWOOSH!!** That's the not-so-subtle fake sound you hear when there's breaking news on TV or a sports score alert. (Or when any other event that some wandering poet editor deems important tickers across the TV screen.)

But it's worse than that. Now almost all news has become "breaking news." Every story is "developing." Multiple irrelevant background visuals are constantly shifting and moving. Super clear HD videos of weather events are purposefully degraded to look like ancient archives. Even some of the preachers get swept up into this false presentation. They try to exhale real hard when they said "God" and "Holy Spirit." It's all plastic, folks. One writer put it this way; *"Society is dominated by the inane notion that action is the only reality."*[124] Can't we all easily see how this is a threat to meaning? Don't you want your existence to have meaning? It's bizarre on the face of it that we're even asking these questions.

77

**Q** *is for In***Q***uisition.* This is what the Christians used to do to the heretics (*1200-1500*). Now it's what the heretics do to the Christians (*1962-2012*). Guess it's just another form of "blowback."

The beginning of the current inquisition can be traced at least as far back as July 10-21, 1925, to the Rhea county courthouse in Dayton, TN. The sham media circus that occurred there is now commonly known as the Scopes Monkey Trial.

**R** *is for* **R***ecount.* *1969 & 2000.* There were 500,000 Frisbee throwers at Woodstock. Not a single baseball kid. So they all became Democrats. There was one anomaly, though. One couple got a little too close in the primordial ooze and produced an illegitimate son. They named him Chadwick PeaceandLove Joplin-Hendrix.

When he was 10, Chad made the cut on his Little League base-ball team. He went on to apply himself in school, get an entry level job, and work real hard to pay off his student loans. Then he moved up the ladder, and was promoted to the home office. West Palm Beach, Florida.

Chad became a thorn in the side of the chattering class when they learned he voted Republican in 2000. They feigned nau-sea, threw some dirt into the air, and said "No Way! Seize that man's ballot!" But the Supreme Court still had enough residual common sense (and Katherine Harris[125] had enough testoster-one) to put the whiners in their place. They never got over it. Even today, ten years later, they're still obsessed with hanging Chad.

**R** *is just too valuable a letter to use only once, so it's included in* **V,S,T,R***.* These letters, taken together, form the perfect destructive liberal storm: **V,S,R,T** *are for* **V***ictimhood,* **S***elf-esteem,* **T***olerance, and* **R***evisionism.*

***Victimhood*** We all have defining events in our lives.  Some are positive; a lot are negative.  One person's abuse is another's challenge.  The difference between an ordeal and an adventure is attitude.  We cannot be a victim unless we choose to be one.  Bob Marley spoke the truth: *None but ourselves can free our minds.*[126]

Promoting an attitude of victimhood in others prevents their growth into maturity by helping them blame decent, hardworking people for everything negative in the "victims" lives.  Creating this illusion helps foster bitterness, hate, and jealousy.  And we thus help the "victims" adopt an illusion of injustice out of common, everyday events.  The three prime instigators are Saul Alinsky,[127] Community Agitators and Cory B. Trotz (a typical wrongful injury lawyer).

***Self-esteem*** Self-esteem is both good and useful.  However, *plastic* self-esteem is very bad.   It can't help but be destructive to psychological well-being.  You can hand out all the accolades and diplomas you like, but if someone can't read or write, or even spell their name on an employment application, you are creating serious internal personal problems.  Trying to picture what all this will mean way on down the road gets a bit nebulous.   It's just an alarmist's prediction, but I'd suggest joining the increasing number of Americans who are stocking up on ammunition  and riot gear.

***Tolerance*** Tolerance is also a great idea.  But in the progressives' world it's just a haughty misnomer, because it's a one way street.  This is bastardized tolerance, and it exists in a pathetic world where good is coerced to tolerate the bad, while bad is not required to tolerate good.   That's not anywhere close to being truly "tolerant."

I'm collecting data in an effort to quantify intolerance.  It would be greatly appreciated, as well as instructive, if you would hold your place here and use just a moment of your time to take the AMP test (Appendix A).

**Revisionism** is a process that rewrites the past by creating illusions that become necessary because of *V,S,T*. We noted how some have created victimhood out of thin air, promoted artificial self-esteem, and tolerated everything except common decency and morality. The whole enterprise is very fragile, and will implode in the real world. So a meaningless, artificial alternate world has to be created. In order to do this, language must be co-opted, Wikipedia must be continually modified, and history must be revised.

Now we're going to witness a story of how things go when *V,S,T* all come together requiring some *R.* And we're all going to see why this is process is a sociological disaster.

I want to introduce everybody to a wonderful Memphis family. Meet Samson Jones and his wife Delilah. Sam was born in Kinshasa. Delilah in Brazzaville. When they were only babies their parents immigrated to the US. Both families settled in Atlanta. Both Samson and Delilah went to college at Spelman. They met in a chemistry class as they studied their way to engineering degrees. About a month after graduation they got married. I think the wedding was about ten years ago.

The Joneses live in an upscale Germantown neighborhood. They have a great family, great career jobs, two late model luxury cars, and they are active in their community and their church. And now that you're done meeting the parents, meet their twin children: Freda and Frank. A boy and a girl, ages 8 and 8. All in all, this is exactly the kind of thing Martin Luther King was dreaming about back in 1963.

Last February was significant on two accounts. First because February is Black history month. At Dogwood elementary the twins had been hearing all about their peoples' history.  This year they had been studying from a book called <u>Zora Hurston and the Chinaberry Tree</u>, by William Miller.  Frank's favorite part of the book said this:

> *Zora learned about Africa, the place where she and her people came from.*
>
> *In Africa they had been kings and queens, builders of cities that stood for thousands of years.*
>
> *They worshipped Gods who ruled the sky, the mountains and rivers, the stormy seas.....*

After reading this part of the book, Frank had been getting very excited.

You see, early in his childhood there were some bullies who tortured Frank.  Told him he was a nobody because his family came from Africa.  They said Africa was backward, and primitive and nothing but garbage and jungle.  As you can imagine, all that taunting caused a lot of hurt and all-around bad self-esteem.  Frank was mentally pretty beat up about it for a long, long time.  But after reading all about Zora Hurston, his world was filled with promise and anticipation.

February was also significant because 2/28 was the first day of Spring Break.  That's the day the Joneses flew out of Memphis to go through Amsterdam on their way to Paris for their dream vacation.  Delilah had wanted to go for a long time because she had always heard Paris was the most romantic city on earth.  Samson only recently wanted to go.  For him this was mainly because Delilah would probably get in a romantic mood when she got to Paris.  The twins wanted to go because they wanted to see Euro Disney, the Eiffel Tower, and – believe it or not – Frank really wanted to see the Louvre.

Why the Louvre, Frank? *We learned in school last Thursday that a special room in the museum opened there in 2001 to show all the wonderful African art that was done back when there were kings and queens and empires the likes of which the world has never seen. I've got to see that art and get some pictures so I can finally settle the score with those bullies.*

The flight over was all-nighter. They didn't get much sleep, what with all the excitement and everything. They made the transfer to KLM in Amsterdam, arrived in Paris, and crashed for few hours in the Concorde Lafayette Hotel. They got up for dinner, then tried to sleep some more since by then it was 800PM. Next day the Jonses hit the ground running.

The Eiffel tower was great; heck, all the way up on the 3$^{rd}$ etage it was *awesome*. Euro Disney was great. (Author's note: I've never been to Euro Disney, so I'll just have to rely on what the Joneses told me.) The romance was great for both Samson and Delilah. A lot of other stuff happened – and there were all kids of wines and baguettes and cheeses. And then came the moment Frank had been waiting for: The Joneses entered the Louvre.

It was HUGE! There was art from everywhere, and it was all over everywhere. The family was really focused on getting Frank where he wanted to go, but to get there they had to go through the Greek and Roman marble sculptures and the Renaissance paintings. All these objects d'art were incredible. But they kept wondering "where is the Africa exhibit?" Finally they got to the end of one of the halls and descended some stairs into a basement. At this point they were trying to hold back the perception that this part of the museum was only a cheap after-thought.

Just before turning a corner to enter the small exhibit room, the Joneses all paused and read a plaque. It said a lot of things in French, but it was also translated into English. Part of it said:

*On 13 April, 2000, French president Jacque Chirac inaugurated the rooms......dedicated to African, Oceanic, Asian, and American Art.*

*The arrival – or rather the return – to the Louvre of this art so long and so unjustly considered as primitive was the fulfillment of the dream of many men over more than a century.*

*A selection of approximately 100 works of exceptional quality.......is thus available to the public..........*

Frank read the plaque.  He could hardly wait to get inside the room and see this fabulous art.  He remembered what the bullies told him – that there was no more backward place on earth than Africa.  He was excited that finally he

 would personally witness some of the great works of art from his family's homeland.  He was going to take some pictures and show those bigoted rednecks that his ancestors were anything but "primitive."

He walked into the room, and the "non-primitive" sculpture to the right was the most magnificent piece he saw.

Now you've got to remember that Frank had just witnessed the greatest art in the history of the world.  From what he'd read back home, he expected no less in this room.  He was very disappointed.  And when he realized that the African piece was from the 19th century AD, and Winged Victory was from 200 BC, he was shattered.  He felt just like Ralphie felt when the secret decoder revealed that all the secret code from Little Orphan Annie was nothing but a crummy Ovaltine commercial.[128]

8 year olds are pretty sharp. Sometimes they get it when even Jacque Chirac doesn't get it. Frank didn't even bother to take the picture. He went back into a funk, and stayed that way for the rest of the trip. He knew there was no way he was going to be able to hold his head up back on the Dogwood Elementary School playground.

The obvious point is this: Racist rednecks have always behaved like idiots, and they've caused a lot of grief. But R,V,S,T is not how to solve the problem. Reformers can spin, redefine, and rewrite all they want. They can ridicule and boycott, and finally silence the real truth-seekers. But in the end, when finally confronted with reality, revisionism will always prove itself incompetent and incapable of maintaining the charade. This is just one of the things wrong with using victimhood, artificial self-esteem, and the lie of tolerance to implement some radical's idea of a utopian future world. There is no more futile a process. Finally, at some point the illusion will be shattered. What then?

*U* is for *U*sama bin Muhammad bin 'Awad bin Ladin, or something like that. At least that's what Wikipedia says. AKA Osama. The letter "O" was just begging to be used by bin Laden, but sadly, it was already taken by Barack bin Hussein bin Obama. Bear with me; it gets confusing and all these Muslim names kinda run together.

Obama, I mean Osama, I mean Usama, had been plotting for about ten years about how he would attack America. He had a campsite set up in the Afghanistan mountains, and was keeping up to date on world affairs by sending carrier pigeons back and forth to the one of the internet cafés over in Kabul. Taking advantage of the benefits of a free and open democratic society he somehow got a plan together, and somehow all the players were in place. It was only left to recognize the optimum time to launch the mission.

On September 8, 2001, Usama received a message. It reported that the US Marines had caved to a flood of emails sent by women in the Corps. These emails were demanding that women be allowed to wear make-up while wearing the battle uniform.[129] This otherwise obscure event was the defining moment for bin Laden.

"Make-up for combat Marines? *Women Marines?* What a bunch of wusses....next thing you know they'll be building gender-neutral aircraft carriers," Usama chuckled. He figured the West was ripe for the picking — that they couldn't get much softer than this. So he stuck a 3M post-it note to the claw of his best pigeon and launched it in the direction of the internet café. The message was secretly forwarded to cell group operatives in The US. The message said "Operation 72 Virgins is GO." Three days later the plan was almost flawlessly executed. September 11, 2001.

You recently may have heard that the Navy Seals took out Usama. This came after Obama (the president) sat for months on the intelligence giving Usama's (the crook) location.[130] Over the vehement objections of Joe Biden, Obama (the president) said the operation could proceed, but only as long as the Seals were under strict orders to exercise "courageous restraint" and bring zero harm to anyone.[131] This was the new vision for war in the "hope and change" world.

The operation was executed. In the ongoing war on terror, this was another "mission accomplished." Reports say bin Laden was shot. After all, his body *was* hauled out and photographed with two apparently deadly bullet wounds. But inside information tells a different story. He actually had a stroke. Here's how it happened: The Seals broke into the compound, and their team leader shouted "MR BIN LADEN, LAY DOWN! WE WILL NOT HARM YOU OR YOUR FAMILY! YOU HAVE THE RIGHT TO REMAIN SILENT. YOU HAVE A RIGHT TO AN ATTORNEY. BLAH, BLAH, BLAH......" And now we all know the complete, unvarnished truth: Usama died laughing.

**Wx** *is for weather.* The biggest weather event in history was Noah and the Flood. Remember the story? The world became so perverse that God destroyed almost all humanity in a great flood. But He graciously brought one family safely through the floodwaters in an ark. And then promised all of us He would never do the flood thing again. And then put a splash of colors up in the sky to seal the promise. And Noah said "OMG! That's beautiful! Look at that!" (BTW, this was the only time, *ever*, that "OMG" was used in a way that didn't violate the Third Commandment. We need to lose that phrase.)

So what do we have today? The most decadent among us have trashed His gift. Now the rainbow's been co-opted into a gay-pride flag. Sexual perversions are back in style, and this time the humans are saying "In your face, God! I'll show you a rainbow!" (Next thing you know they'll create an angelic rainbow halo to honor Barack Hussein Obama for his ambiguous support of oxymoronic same-sex marriage. Oh wait, that's already happening.[132])

*Segue alert #1.* There's another angle to this story........another chapter about what man becomes when he embraces perversity and decadence. Sodom and Gomorrah. The story line here is that local homosexuals were trying to get dates with Lot's house guests and were struck blind. Now get this: Even after the life changing catastrophe of sudden blindness, *they were still trying to find Lot's door.*[133]

> **Nimrod**: "Uncle Elihu.......I can't see.... Oh no, I'm blind!"
> **Elihu**: "Shut up Nimrod.....Say, are you near Lot's house? Speak up so I can find those pretty boys!"
> **Nimrod**: "What's it gonna be: Shut up, or Speak up? And anyway, how will we get home?"
> **Elihu**: (grumbling) "Doesn't matter, now where's that door?"

Uncle Elihu may have been the Bible's first prophet, 'cause going home really didn't matter. In just a few hours the whole neighborhood went "poof," and disappeared in smoke.

Now think about the modern problem of AIDS in the context of this story. No, I'm not saying God brought AIDS to homosexuals as punishment. Nobody can prove that either way. There's something else that's obvious and undeniable in both ancient Sodom and the modern gay community. A simple, unavoidable observation: *Even when a sin or a disease is destroying some people, they still seek ways to persist in the behavior that brought the destruction.* They still are consumed with "trying to find the door" – *even when they've been blinded!*

*Segue alert #2.* Another Bible lesson. The reference for this one is 1 John 1:6-7:

> *If we say that we have fellowship with Him, and walk in darkness, we lie and do not practice the truth. But if we walk in the light as He is in the light, we have fellowship with one another, and the blood of Jesus Christ His Son cleanses us from all sin.*

Every human being – each of us -- has a choice. We can choose to walk in the light, or choose to walk in darkness. A key question for us is "How does one choose to walk in the light?" Let's explore the answer. Try to remember one of the key points from chapter 7. Recall that The One who created us gave us the User's Guide. The Guide tells us how to find spiritual life, and it tells us how to physically live. As long as we revere the concepts given in God-breathed words found in The Guide, we will be walking in the light. In other words, it's like walking across the living room with the lights on. But if we disrespect God's word by refusing its counsel, we will have then made a choice to walk in darkness. And we won't be able to cross the room. Application? The Guide says any sex other than that practiced in heterosexual marriage is wrong. That's a very simple obvious truth. But the selfish interests of a lot of people force many of them to ultimately proclaim "The Guide is a Fable! The Guide doesn't know what it's like to be me!" By doing this they kill God in their own minds and proclaim themselves sovereign. But what they have practically done is reached their hand out to the switch and turned off the light.

People's life choices commit them to something. Anything we commit to totally will become the sum of our lives -- our whole identity. It could be drugs or nicotine or sex or.......Jesus. It may be little by little, or perhaps in one fell swoop, but we all make our choice.

### *Y* is for *"You Can't Be Serious, Man. You Cannot Be Serious!"*[134]

This section is brought to you by the letter *Y*. *Y* is tasked with being the catch-all for a lot of loose ends. Here come the machine gun sound bites that couldn't fit anywhere else. Hey, even the word processor is in on the imagery; it calls them "bullet points." (Wonder how long before the PC police outlaw "bullet points"? It won't be too long after that until it won't be necessary for the left to outlaw the 2nd amendment. Everyone will be going "What's a bullet? What's a gun?" Unfortunately, they'll also be asking "What's America?")

It's hard to tell if these points portray a tragedy or a comedy. Guess it depends on whether you're the actor or the audience. Or maybe it depends on whether it describes entertainment or describes life. It's necessary to warn the reader that with all the randomness, it'll be hard to maintain focus. Try to remember that these realities and potential realities point to the destruction of the West through the death of meaning. Enjoy (sarcasm).

➢ Someone has decided that it's OK for yesterday's men/ women to become today's women/men, with nothing to stop them from defaulting back to their original operating systems tomorrow. I'm OK, you were OK, you are OK, you will be OK. This ridiculously absurd chaos is going on while some "thinkers" are insisting there's no difference between the sexes. It doesn't appear that progressive intellectuals have thought this thing all the way through. Don't they realize that it's now legally and theoretically impossible to commit sexual harassment, since it's impossible to know what sex anyone is anymore?

> *Your Honor, I know the joke about women was crude and I am deeply sorry. But please take into consideration the fact that we were in the men's shower, and that she was still a man up until about 3 seconds before I gave the punch line. I didn't even know he was a woman until I got this court summons. Heck, even he didn't know he was a she until one second after he became one.*

➤ Perhaps we've all had a chance to listen to computer-generated NOAA weather on the radio. These broadcasts are the ones with mechanically synthesized voices. Pay close attention next time, and remember these are *computer generated* voices. Notice that the broadcasts are split exactly 50/50 between *synthetic* male and female voices. How did that happen? Did the female data bytes sue for equal opportunity exposure? Doesn't everybody know that the male voice is the only one authorized to do the weather? Don't people know that white Western males invented the weather? What planet am I on?

We may as well go all the way with this kind of folly. Ever notice that batteries have two terminals, positive (+) and negative (-)? And did you also notice that the positive ones are the *male* end, while the negative ones are *female*? How much bad karma has that caused?

In a similar vein, the negative leads on car batteries are *black*. So why do females and blacks have to always be labeled "negative"? Maybe we can bring about some closure for the traumatized weaklings on this planet by making exactly 50% of all batteries with opposite polarization. And by making half the black car battery leads "positive." How will we know which is which? That's easy. Just connect the wires to the battery, and if you've got it wrong you'll know real quick. But get out some burn cream first.

➤ The Seattle Times June 2, 2011. A stand-alone quote:

> *A gay softball organization can keep its rule limiting the number of heterosexual players on each team, but allegations by three players who say they were disqualified from a tournament because they weren't gay enough can proceed to trial, a federal judge said.*
>
> *Three men claim in a lawsuit filed last year that their team's second place finish in the 2008 tournament in Washington state was nullified because they are bisexual, not gay, and thus their team exceeds the limit of two non-gay players.*

➤ Or that Apple computer thing. You know, the iconic graphic of an apple with a bite out of it. Supposed to symbolize man's quest for technological access to more and more knowledge. But the original implication of the bitten apple was *fallen humanity*. I may be the only one, but it seems to me like it's the worst kind of stretch to portray man's advancement with a symbol of his fall. But, wait a minute..........I'm sorry....... did you say "byte"? I thought it was "bite." My bad

➤ The Nobel Peace Prize has become increasingly meaningless. It was awarded to Carter, then Gore, then Obama. Bad, Worse, Worst. Looks like the only criteria now is that you have to know how to breathe and maybe say "I care." (But this one's easy to understand: Basically it's now awarded to Frisbee throwers by other Frisbee throwers.)  A Dr. Katz[135] episode is helpful here.  His patient says:

> *You know doctor; I used to think the human brain was the most amazing thing in the universe.  But then I realized something:  Look what's telling me that!*

➢ Men married men; women married women; and so marriage became meaningless.  What did anybody expect?

➢ There are now graduation ceremonies for every grade, including daycare, Pre-K and K.  A glimmer of hope:  There haven't been any formal graduations from the maternity wards (so far).

➢ Little League Baseball:  In a lot of towns there are now no cuts, there are no outs, every player plays every minute, and everyone gets a MVP trophy.  And of course there's no score-keeping.  But even the Frisbee throwers have to admit (don't they?) that games without scoring are obviously *pointless*, don't they?  Bueller?  Bueller?

➢ The Chattering Class decided it couldn't stand the "D" in "AD."  Or the "C" in "BC."  So they changed them to "BCE" and "CE."  It's so patently silly.  When Western Culture was sane, the reference point of our existence was chosen.  The years still count toward, and away from, that same point.  Besides, what are we going to say when the 3rd graders ask,

> *Mommy, mommy.....2010 years from when?*

> *Erica, I've told you a million times it's since the beginning of the Current Era.*

> *But, mommy.......What's the "Current Era" mean?  Wasn't that when Jesus was born?*

*ERICA! Wash your mouth!!! Where did you hear about JESUS??? I know it wasn't in school! Was it Schwartz[136] who told you that?*

➢ And now there's some kind of problem with "GMT" (Greenwich Mean Time). Apparently the world couldn't stand it that lines of longitude, and therefore all clocks, were referenced to the Royal Observatory in Greenwich, England. So "GMT" had to become "UTC" (Coordinated Universal Time). OK, so they changed the name -- so what? World time is still referenced to the same point. Except now there's a movement afoot to have the Prime Meridian pass through Mecca, of all places.

*At a conference in Doha in 2008, Muslim clerics and scholars presented 'scientific' arguments that Makkah time is the true global meridian. They said that Makkah is the center of the world.[137]*

So it's like the Muslims got their feelings hurt, and now we have to spin the whole globe exactly 39 degrees 49' 34" to the West so they can get some closure. In the "mean time", it's going to be hilarious when the Saudia Airline pilots try to program Mecca's longitude as 0 degrees into their navigation computers. If you dial the numbers in on Google Earth, you'll see where they'll be headed. It's a lovely spot in the desert just over the Algerian border in northeastern Mali.

➢ I know this is laughable, but people have actually said -- with straight faces -- that "substance follows form." The 180 degree shift away from "form follows substance" was a disaster for Christianity. It led to the dark ages. Historical inertia carries many of those 1000 year-old ills into our spiritual lives today. Furthermore, we haven't learned our lesson from history. We're being set up again, this time for a cultural "Dark Age."  Some are given to swooning and call-ing the coming nightmare the "Age of Aquarius."  They need to get off the sauce and smell the coffee.

➢ The Academy Awards became a political venue for gays to give awards to gays for writing scripts in which gay actors portrayed persecuted gays.  And the fingernails on the chalkboard get excruciatingly loud when we have to sit through some Broadway productions.  These are where gay dancers try to act out an atheist playwright's interpretation of man praising God. (Ever see Riverdance?) Or Bill Clinton gets out the BIG Bible to deflect the Lewinsky rumors in his staged church photo-op.  Or Ricky Martin comes out of the closet to sing a love cha-cha-cha to some Latin beauty.  Or Barbara Streisand sings "O Little Town of Bethlehem."  Or Michael Buble sings "Silent Night."  Or Meryl Streep pre-tends to be Margaret Thatcher.  Or Barack Hussein Obama's mouth actually forms the words "God bless America."

➢ Next thing you know some parents will make the unbeliev-able but inevitable all-in commitment to this wonderful Age of Aquarius and begin raising their children to be gender-neutral.  Oh wait...... that's already happening.[138]

➢ Next thing you know, some peer-reviewed Eco-Socio-Justice professor will begin working to re-brand legitimate scientific dissent about man-caused global warming.  It'll be re-branded it as a "mental disorder requiring pharmacological or psycho-logical treatment."  Oh, wait......that's already happening.[139]

➢ Next thing you know, someone will say that the expression of personal Bible-based beliefs about "lesbian, gay, bisex-ual, transgender, intersex and queer" practices is "violence."  Oh, wait.......that's already happening.[140]  (Did I hear some-one say "Hate Crime"?)

➢ Next thing you know, someone will push for legislation approving the murder of babies born live during attempted abortions. Oh, wait.......that's already happening.[141] (If you aren't overcome with revulsion and shame to the point of tears when you see this footnoted YouTube video, you've lost the name you're called by. IOW, you've lost your humanity.)

➢ Next thing you know, the intellectuals will begin arguing that there's now no "moral" difference between an unborn and a newborn, removing all "moral" barriers to infanticide. Oh, wait........that's already happening.[142]

➢ Next thing you know, someone's going to censor this book. Oh, wait....

➢ "Celebrate Diversity" never had any meaning because it was only meant to apply to fringe behavior. IOW, it wasn't diverse enough to include to the vast, decent majority. Now we're learning that the intention all along was really "Celebrate Perversity." Proof: the diversity celebrators have only contempt for God-fearing, heterosexual, Christian, white, male, 2nd amendment gun owners. They feel this way about any normal American, for that matter. Some extremists even say these people "get bitter" and that "they cling to guns or

religion or antipathy to people who aren't like them." No kidding, some people have actually said that.

But, here's a sacred cross. Let's stick it in a jar of urine. Wow -- That's cool! And here's a picture of William Ayers, desecrating the American flag. Let's celebrate him! I know he bombed the Pentagon, and he also tried to kill some of the decent people, but let's give him a professorship. HOW STUPID IS THAT? (Celebrate Diversity will continue to be meaningless at least until there are the same numbers of conservative and liberal professors.)

➢ Science in general and weather in particular is trending toward meaninglessness. Here's a comparison of typical weather maps used for TV news reports in the US and in Europe. For you people who are recent products of the NEA through American public schools, the US map is the one on the left. Now which of these maps is more scientifically accurate and useful? Which one is geared toward "feelings"? Can you guess where American "science" is headed?

 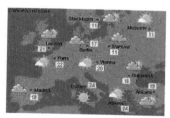

**Z** *is for* **ZZZZZZZZZZZZZZZZZZ**.

The majority of Americans are comfortable in their own skin. They merely wish for a peaceful culture where they can go about their business of working, playing, and contributing to the good of humanity. Maybe they'll raise a family. Most of them praise their Creator. These are the decent people. But these decent people need to wake up, or there's going to be no decency left on the planet.

This brings us to the end. We're finished with the rise and fall of America. America is probably finished, too.

You may have noticed I used a really weird alphabet. I thought it up all by myself.

## *AB 'CDDEFG  H/I   J J M/L/K (M) NO 0 PPQR  V/S/T/R UWxYZ.*

Excuse me?  You got a problem with this alphabet?  Who's to say it's not reality?  Modern intellectuals, in their infinite wisdom, have insisted there are absolutely no absolutes.  Therefore my collection of letters is just as valid as any other alphabet.  Besides, the traditional English arrangement is probably just another subtle but powerful form of English/American imperialism.  There seems to be a lot of agitators who think they've been psychologically "imperialized." These poor, tortured souls need some closure.  So just consider my alphabet as a meager contribution to the cause of "Social Justice."

# 13 The Big Ending

We've arrived ingloriously at our finale. This finale probably was the whole point from the beginning, and I mean the beginning of time, because the "conspiracy" is probably more supernatural than natural. Bottom line: Humanity ignored its reference point, lost its identity, and became meaningless. This result becomes inevitable anytime Man puts himself in place of God – anytime the creature pretends to be the Creator. (Read Romans 1:18-32. But don't read it out loud, because all those idealists pushing "tolerance" will probably arrest you right in your own church. To them your views reflect an unacceptable kind of diversity. So I guess there really are diversity police. This clues us in to a dirty little secret: The conservative man's diversity is the progressive man's intolerance.)

Other poets have lamented our plight:

> In other times, in other lives
> I'd have read you books of poetry --
> Or at least a line from Browning.
>
> But the Earth has died and love is fear,
> And no one cares to linger here --
> At least no one to speak of.

Caught fast in webs of cyber fire,
Hypnotic waves of light,
The souls of men await their fate
Subdued by voiceless powers

In other times, in other lives,
I'd pray with you before this meal --
And then we'd share our future.

But the moon is dark, the sun is pale,
And this cold world resembles Hell --
Or at least a trackless ocean.

Caught shelterless before the storm --
Anchorless and blind,
The souls tied to the ship's foremast
Have lost their sense of sight;
Or at least the name they're called by.[143]

You probably haven't heard about the new iPhone app. That's OK, not many people are aware of it. It looks like the regular calendar app, but it's so much more than a simple calendar. It's called the "Prophecy" app. This new program allows the user to spin a time wheel to any future date, touch "enter," and then operate informationally as if the chosen date is the current date. By doing this, it's possible to see what has actually happened (or happens?) in the world between the present "now" and the chosen "now."

Let's do one exercise for practice. Dial in January 28, 2016, and press "enter." The main headline says the whole earthly population is coming back out of caves and shelters and resuming normal life. They were convinced that everything was going to be consumed by fire. You see, AlGore prophesied on January 27, 2006 that the Earth had just ten years until environmental Armageddon. Note that most of the bloggers on this date are trying to figure out if this was a display of incompetence, insanity, or just the most expensive joke ever told.

OK, now we're up to speed on using the App.  Next we're going to dial in October 7, 2018, touch "enter."  Then select the "Drudge Report" icon.  Let's see whassup.  (But be careful; if we overshoot that date by a couple of years we'll find there's no "Drudge Report."  And no "Fox" icon.  There will only be NPR, CNN, NBC, CBS, ABC, and BBC.  And all of them will be saying the same thing, because they'll be having their news supplied from the unilaterally appointed White House News Czar, Debbie Wasserman Shultz.)

If you're like me and you're a sports fan, the first headline that catches your eye will be the one saying "One year anniversary of the final game of the final World Series."  What with all the food foraging, and going to the well to pump some water, and the bread making and climbing up and down stairs in the downtown communal high rise, it appears that the people in the future will completely forget about baseball.

A lot of this information has to come from blogs, because the official news outlets are disappointingly sketchy.  It winds up being a vague guess, but this is what appears to have happened:  Baseball's death was a two-step process.  First, the wandering poets got together, boycotted the beer companies, signed a petition, and then presented it to the Ex-Right Honorable Maud Wilson.  They complained that it was unconstitutional to sing the national anthem because it said "God."  The decent people who loved baseball, and God and country pointed out that nobody says "God" when they sing the national anthem.  This is where Maud Wilson weighed in (by now she carried a lot of weight) and said it was wrong to argue about the meaning of words. And then she petitioned her friends at the 9th Circuit to rule the National Anthem unconstitutional.  They complied, citing again – you guessed it – the "principle of Social Justice."  (One of the petitioning atheists hadn't slept for ten years because he thought he heard "God" in the anthem.  He needed some closure.)

The 9<sup>th</sup>'s ruling was appealed all the way to the top and then upheld by the Star Wars Bar. That ruling was a foregone conclusion because Barack Hussein Obama had emulated FDR's insane desire to pack the court (except Obama succeeded) by appointing two additional Supreme Court Judges. This brought the total to 11. That's 7 permanent Frisbee throwers. That's "Change" all right, but it's not "Hope." -- In fact, it's *Hopeless Change*. And at that point every legal appeal had become a fraud; basically just a rubber-stamp process. And every pretense of checks and balances was banished forever. Boy, if that's where we're headed, it definitely looks hopeless. Cry for the children.

But back to the game of baseball itself; it disappeared, but only after a thousand lacerations in the form of "human-interest-stories." The moment of death was October 7th, 2017. It was the bottom of the ninth in the seventh game of the World Series, score tied. Rodriguez Rodriguez (Rod-Rod) was up to pinch-hit for the Atlanta Force. (They used to be the Braves, but the decent people turned coward and caved.)

Anyway, the network chose this crucial point in the game to go to that season's 1000<sup>th</sup> human interest story. It was a canned presentation about Rod-Rod's fourth cousin's teenage daughter from Haiti who had a severely cleft upper lip since birth. (Nathaniel Watson, Jr. had been saving this story since the Port-au-Prince earthquake.) By the time the network got back to the game there was a Viagra commercial and no one saw the end. We still don't know who won. And we don't know what happened to baseball. You turn on the TV and all you see are tobacco commercials that tell you not to smoke, beer commercials that tell you not to drink, medical stuff to enlarge the Baby-boomer's experiences. And BP commercials that tell you not to drive. And, oh yeah, Anderson Cooper's tear-jerker poems and human-interest-stories. Everything's metro-sexualized or chickified. Maybe they're still playing baseball. It really doesn't matter / who cares?

Wow......can things really disappear that easily? A frantic Google search in this new iPhone app reveals that a lot of other things are not going to look the same in 7 or 8 years. ("Google" in the blogosphere came/will come to mean "**G**overnment **O**verseers **O**rder **G**iant **L**ies for

Everything.  But Eric Holder decided/will decide that the bloggers' satire was going too far.  He decided/will decide that any dissent was/is racial hatred.  He clamped/will clamp down on the bloggers.  Some of them are/were/will be serving 10-year jail time for Hate Thought crimes.)

Let's dial the "Prophecy" app ahead two more years.  2020.  Do a Google search for "Sports."  There's not much there.  If a search is done for key words Babe Ruth, Jackie Robinson, Mickey Mantle, or Hank Aaron all that shows is......nothing.

The only sports story that comes up in this "now" is the one about the All-Time, All-Star Softball Team.  It's tough to tell much about the photo of the team if you're reading this on your iPhone.  I suggest going to the iPad for more detail.  It's reproduced on the next page for your inspection.

# ALL-TIME, ALL-STAR SOFTBALL TEAM

**FRONT ROW, LEFT TO RIGHT**: Janet Napolitano, Melissa Etheredge, Rosie O'Donnell, Jane Lynch.

**SECOND ROW**: Merideth Baxter, Ruth "Buzzy" Ginsberg, Janet El Reno, Hillary Rodham Clinton, Wanda Sykes, Cammermeyer (Sir!)

**BACK ROW:** Information Director - the Ferret-like Paul Krugman. Elena Kagan, Rene Richards, Rachel Maddow, Ellen Degeneres, BJ King, KD Lang. Head Coach – William Jefferson "Bear" Clinton.

The softball team pictured above was the brainchild of Paul Krugman. He decided to get all these players together to celebrate the Chattering Class's triumph over decency, morality, and all things honorable.

So, the National Anthem was banned, then Baseball died, then sports history was rewritten, then the rest of history was rewritten, then there was no more meaning, and then there was no more America. If we had to choose one pivotal event which triggered all this destruction, it would arguably have to be when Joseph McCarthy and Richard Nixon tried to tell a bunch of slimy leftist they couldn't have their candy way back in 1948.

PS -- If the iPhone prophecy app is spun forward as fast as it will go, it stops abruptly on the year 2525. And that's where you find this pitiful postscript to human existence:

> *Captain's Log, Star Date 1/27/2525:* *Encountered planet Solar3. Aka: "Earth". Mostly jungle and some desert with varied non-intelligent life forms. Rich, inexhaustible mineral deposits. Decaying evidence of extinct advanced intelligence. This civilization appears to have gone into suicide mode by refusing to harvest plentiful life-sustaining resources, by abandoning obvious universal standards for decency, and by glorifying the basest kind of living.*

> *Found: Time capsule bearing the logo "Sierra Club", dated 2020 CE, and containing the following mission statement.*

>> *It is our goal to work with Green Peace and use whatever means necessary, including civil disobedience and guerilla terrorism, to prevent human life-forms from affecting any natural facet of Mother Earth.*

>> *Our Motto: Forget the Humans -- Remember the Snail Darter!*

> *Also found: Thousands of copies of the "User's Guide" locked away in a sealed vault, guarded by statues of gargoyle angels with fiery swords. Appears that the*

*offending word in the guide was "God." The offending phrase was "Subdue the Earth." If followed, these guides would have provided for an optimum existence. The decision to confiscate these books appears to mark the point of no return in an insane slide toward self-annihilation.*

***Recommended Star Fleet Mission:*** *Dispatch harvester fleet to tap estimated 800-year supply of oil, coal, and natural gas.*

# Epilogue:  Hungarian Rhapsody

To chain yourself to a desk and bang away on a word processor -- this is a despicable, but apparently necessary preoccupation. You have to act like a chattering class person. But everybody ought to try it at least once. We need to do

what we can to save Western Civilization. We need more little Dutch boys; we need to plug up the dike.

Here's how it goes: Set up shop for a week in a Paris hotel.  Open up the windows.  Sit long hours at a desk.  Sip some wine and nibble some cheese.  Get all self-absorbed and involved with your intellect.  Begin manipulating a few words and trying to shape a few thoughts, all under the guise of enlightening other minds.  Inherent in the process is the idea that other minds don't know what you know.  But that's just a self-deception.  C. S. Lewis may have said it best: "We read to know we're not alone." Another way of looking at it: You're not creating -- you're just trying to uncover what's already there. And maybe describe it from a different angle.

Now your brain is starting to chatter. Like Hemingway, Mailer, or Stein (well, sort of....). Or even like the ferret-like Paul Krugman. And while you're wordsmithing along it's tempting to think your contribution to society is more important than, say, the man who's going to do the oil change on your car when you get back home. But you're just a looter -- he's the one paying your ticket. He deserves the honor, 'cause he's way more Nobel.

Half-way through the final draft comes a change in venue. Now it's a hotel suite in Budapest overlooking the Danube. Across the river a massive fort looms high on a hill. Your body is still sweat soaked from a climb up that mountain. Words flow out of fingers as thoughts return to the trail.

In other times it would've been easy to just run up to the top. But 7 years of inactivity and 2 bouts with pulmonary emboli have redefined your physical limits. It takes a lot of effort just to walk twenty steps & pause, walk & pause. And as you struggled with that, you struggled with how to close the circle on this book.

Put that struggle in the back of your mind because here at the top is an incomparable sight. It's well worth the effort. Budapest spreads out in a spectacular vista. You wonder how history moved through this place. You forgot to get the Fodor's. And Wikipedia is on your computer -- way down there, across that bridge, up an elevator to the fourth floor of that gray building.

And then a gift: A British tour group pauses within earshot. The guide reveals himself to be a native of this city. His English is accented, but not heavily so. He's obviously proud of his speaking ability. Proud in a good way.

*1918*: Couldn't hear all of it; something about a failed 133 day revolution. *1945*: Retreating Nazis try to destroy the city. *1946*: Communists

106

take over. *1989*: The Iron Curtain goes away, and *2010*: My accidental guide is speaking in English to a group of Brits on formerly forbidden soil. He is also obviously very proud of his city.

He was 18 in 1989, living in Budapest. He remembers vividly how life was before liberation. The fear. The curse that you couldn't speak your mind. The horror when some of his friends and a few of his relatives simply vanished. He says that when one of his cousins disappeared, no one in his family ever said a word about it. He says they had to "live every minute of every day as if the walls had ears." (His words, not mine.).

And this man is not one bit ambivalent about Freedom. Without a hint of apology, almost in tears, he lets his group know how much he reveres the great US president, Ronald Reagan.

At this point your thoughts turn toward home as you begin musing about where American culture is headed. It's easy to get lost in pseudo-facts as the American chattering class revises history. They want to fool us into believing the demise of Communist Russia was at best a net draw. But you don't need a revised history book, dumbed down to Ebonics and approved by the NEA, to know the truth. Not if you're in Budapest, or Prague, or Warsaw, or East Berlin. Anyone in those cities who was at least 10 years old in 1989 will gladly show you the way.

Budapest is as far as the tether will stretch. In two days, Memphis will begin reeling me in. Barcelona, Dublin, Atlanta, and then home. It's painful to admit, but I know I'm returning to a culture that does not know it has checked itself into an asylum. The slippery slope must surely be near vertical. Maybe there's still more to do than simply pray. Maybe we can still share the truth. We can share the truth until truth is banned. And I also urge you to do this: When you witness an event or statement that goes against the grain of common decency, SPEAK UP! You should do it in a Christ-like way using respect and reasonable demeanor. And take comfort and encouragement from the fact that the decent people are still in the majority in America. We need to make our presence known.

Budapest is still hiding all kinds of meaning, and it's about to reveal one more poignant lesson. Later that day, after the hike and the writing, I get to take a last stroll before going to the airport. Down a street, through Roosevelt Plaza. Around another corner, and here is the Parliament. And here is a curious sight -- a flag with a round hole in its center. It's flies over a granite tombstone and this is what it means: In October 1956 the decent people tried to get their country back. They cut the Soviet coat-of-arms out of the bastardized Hungarian flag and marched their protest right up to the feet of the occupying tyrants. Hundreds of them were executed on that grassy lawn. And today their blood still cries out from their native soil.

An awkwardly translated inscription beneath the flag tells us:

> *This Hungarian flag has a hole in it because on October 23, 1956 the revolutionists, those Hungarian who revolted against the Soviet Union, tore out of it the foreign coat of arms that symbolized the power of the Soviet Union and Communism. Since then this flag has symbolized the freedom of the Hungarian nation.*

*This memorial is a symbolic grave. Here, on this square, several hundreds of people fell dead onto the ground due to the killer blow of a firing squad on October 25, 1956. Honor and remebranche [sic] to the victims!*

I know what you've just finished reading may be overly flippant and irreverent. Some will say it's poorly written (they'd be right). Some will object to the humorous approach. Many others will react to their feelings and say "you sound like a jerk." And at this point I can hear my cousin Melvin's wise words: "It's hard to take you seriously, David." Well, at this point it doesn't much matter, because as we come to the end, the seriousness can't be held back. Perhaps the entertainment has served its purpose and kept your interest. But now it's time to quit entertaining. It's time to recognize that this is darn serious business. (That needs to be said more emphatically than just "darn", but aspirations of decency will not permit the curse.) In Budapest, in front of the Parliament on this beautiful green lawn, the soft summer evening is quietly winding down. But don't be lulled to sleep by the tranquility. Time is short. We must remember the past and wake up to the future's ominous threat. For here, as in so many other similar places, history is screaming the truth -- crying out the obvious to all who will hear:

*When truth is banished, the only way back is blood.*

Time to close this book. Time to pause in prayer. I pray that I am not alone.

Budapest, July 4, 2010

# Appendix A

## The AMP* Test

Rank these four groups in order of your perception of which is most bigoted, intolerant, and judgmental. 1 is the most, and 4 is the least.

_____         White American Males

_____         Middle-Eastern Muslims

_____         American Blacks

_____         Feminists

(*A Guess By You / Monolithic Perceptions Test. Commonly called the "AMP" Test. The test will soon be available online. Results will be collected, tabulated, and presented in the second edition of this book.)

# Appendix B

Here are some excerpts from Sojourners.com staff bios. It's hard to find anyone in this group who has done anything other than put words on paper or cause a big public stink. If you're in a hurry, this will save you the trouble of going to the actual website (these are all quotes):

> .........*bestselling author, public theologian, speaker, and international commentator on ethics and public life. He recently served on the President's Advisory Council on Faith-based and Neighborhood Partnerships and currently serves as the chair of the Global Agenda Council on Faith for the World Economic Forum.*

> ..........*prior to coming to Sojourners, she served for nearly five years as the Chief Administrator for the Office of the Chairman, President and CEO at Enterprise Community Partners.*

> ......... *received a Bachelor of Social Work to provide a foundation for advocating for social change. While in school, her campus Amnesty International organization was a great place for her to join with other individuals who believed in the value of every human life.*

.........holds a B.S. in Community Leadership and Development from Springfield College in Springfield, Massachusetts, and between graduating and beginning work at Sojourners, she worked as a community organizer in New Haven, Connecticut.

.......spent 20 years working as a volunteer on advocacy, activism, justice, faith-based organizing and peace work.

.......has been active as an organizer and administrator in the peace and justice movement for 35 years, beginning as a draft resistance and antiwar organizer during the Vietnam War. He has worked as a community organizer in the rural south, in interfaith coalitions, and in the nuclear weapons freeze and Central America solidarity movements of the 1980s. His positions have included Associate for the National Inter-religious Service Board for Conscientious Objectors; National Coordinator for the Committee Against Registration and the Draft; Deputy Director and Acting Executive Director for SANE/Freeze; and Research Fellow for the Institute for Policy Studies.

.......was the founding executive director of New York Faith & Justice, an organization at the hub of a new ecumenical movement to end poverty in New York City. Her writing has been featured in The National Civic Review, God's Politics blog, The Huffington Post, Urban Faith, Prism, and Slant33 where she has written extensively on tax reform, comprehensive immigration reform, health care reform, poverty, racial justice, and transformational civic engagement.

.......faith-rooted approach to advocacy and organizing has activated people of faith across the U.S. and around

*the world to address structural and political injustice as
an outward demonstration of their personal faith.*

Makes me want to throw up. It's sickening to see how some Christian teachers have allowed themselves to be co-opted by progressivism.

Ever hear of "circular reasoning"? Well, all these kinds of qualifications constitute "circular competence." Contrast them with the qualifications given in the following bio:

> .......*excelled in school, got a nursing degree in two years, worked at four hospitals in three years, quit her profession to raise three children and run an excellent household, taught classes in church, used her experience as a mother and Christian to do volunteer work with disadvantaged minorities in the Memphis inner-city.*

I've just introduced you to my wife. The key words in her bio are *used her experience.* Because of her experience, her counsel is far more instructive, valuable, wise and practical than anything you can get from theoreticians in freeloader organizations, entities, or foundations like Sojourners.

# (Endnotes)

1    Non-linear thinking = "Thinking outside the box." The process is very use-ful for developing the most  possible solutions for any given problem. But, it is absolutely useless when trying to practically implement any kind of solution. The only way to put the best solution into useful practice is to get back inside the box. A sentence has to be written.  An equation has to be used.  2+2 still equals 4.

2    "A theory that involves a radical reappraisal of modern assumptions about culture, history, identity or language."  Merriam-Webster

3    Elizabeth Shue's character in the movie "The Saint."

4    Wikipedia says this about Einstein:   *"Near the beginning of his career, Einstein thought that Newtonian mechanics was no longer enough to reconcile the laws of classical mechanics with the laws of the electromagnetic field.  This led to the development of his special theory of relativity."* (12/31/11)

5    "Yes We're Broke, But Leave the Diversity Machine Alone," John Leo, 10/26/2011.

*"This is an old story on our campuses.  Colleges and universities enact severe budget cuts, dropping programs and letting teachers go, while unapologeti-cally expanding their already swollen diversity bureaucracy.  This is because diversity now has the status of an established religion on our campuses, while actual teaching deals only in mere learning."*

6    Wikipedia, December 29, 2011

7   **Matt Lauer**: *"You have said, I understand, to some close friends, that this is the last great battle, and that one side or the other is going down here."*

**Hillary Clinton**: *"Well, I don't know if I've been that dramatic.  That would sound like a good line from a movie.  But I do believe that this is a battle.  I mean, look at the very people who are involved in this – they have popped up in other settings.  This is --- the great story here for anybody willing to find it and write about it.......... -- is this vast right-wing conspiracy that has been conspiring against my husband since the day he announced for president."* (January 27, 1998)

8   Some of the social changes sought in the '60s were noble and necessary. The effort by students to take over school administrations and dictate curricula was not one of them.

9   Since the John Kerry presidential campaign of 2004, there have been several efforts to "set the record straight" and redefine the protestors' vile actions as merely an urban myth.  One big obstacle to pulling this off is the large number of first-hand accounts given by the Vietnam vets themselves.  Until the Bob Greene book <u>Homecoming: When the Soldiers Returned from Vietnam</u> is finally banned from the public purview, the hippies' shameful actions will be a part of recorded history.

One effort at revising the truth was a <u>Free Republic</u> post by John Llewllyn, *When Vietnam vets came home (Soldiers being spit on is just an urban myth)* 11/10/2004.  Llewllyn tries to make his case by saying "only 3 percent of returning soldiers recounted any unfriendly experiences upon their return."  3 percent sounds at first like an insignificant number.  But one is compelled to ask "3 percent of what?"  3.4 million served in Southeast Asia during the Vietnam era.  That computes into 90,000 cases of abuse.  90,000 first person experiences takes this out of the realm of an urban myth.

10   See footnote 12

11   Here's some evidence that you can't trust Wikipedia for the facts of history. This is one case of probably tens of thousands. On September 11, 2008, Charlie Gibson did a TV interview with Sarah Palin. At one point he asked her to comment on the "Bush Doctrine." Her measured non-response generated an avalanche of media criticism.

There was a problem in this criticism. Neither Gibson, nor anyone else in the media had a firm idea of what the "Bush Doctrine" was. Proof? In the <u>one week</u> following that September interview there were approximately 400 revisions to the Wikipedia article on this topic. In the previous 52 weeks before the interview there was an average of 1.5 revisions per week to the article. A few of the revisions were legitimate. But the vast majority were simply opportunistic spin aiming at making Palin and Bush look foolish. And I wonder how Gibson would've reacted if Palin had brushed him off by saying "Oh, gosh darn Charlie; you know I can't answer that. It's above my pay grade!"

12   I've worked with a lot of pilots who were naval aviation officers. Some of them spent part of their careers involved with the Navy's precision flight team, the Blue Angels. It is common knowledge among this elite group of aviators that Donnie Cochran, the first African American team leader, was asked to resign because of his poor performance as skipper. The Wikipedia article praises the honor and judgment he displayed when he "voluntarily" resigned.

I know first-hand  that attempts have been made to get Wikipedia to more accurately record the facts of history about the Blue Angels and Donnie Cochran. These attempts were rebuffed because the editors said they wanted to post only "positive information." This is fictionalization for the sake of social self-esteem.

13   "To anger a conservative, lie to him.  To anger a liberal, tell him the truth."
Teddy Roosevelt

14   *Against the Wind*, Bob Seger, 1980

15    *Turn the Page*, Bob Seger, 1972

16    Captain Billy Tyne, from *"The Perfect Storm"*

17    Dorothy, after seeing Oz for the first time.  *The Wizard of Oz.*

18    Indiana to Marion in *Raiders of the lost Ark*: *"It's not the years honey, it's the mileage."*

19    The Brits turned Rhodesia into a civilized garden.  It became known as the "Breadbasket of Africa."  But it became Zimbabwe.  Enough said.

20    Now Turkey

21    Now Palestine, Israel, Syria, Jordan and Lebanon

22    Western Thought likely began with Thales of Miletus.  The year, near as we can tell, was 578 BC.  (Philosophy for Beginners, Richard Osborne)

23    April 18, 1522

24    Defeat of the Spanish Armada, August, 1588.

25    1215, 1225, &1297

26    Guess this is an anachronism.  Gatorade was invented in 1965.

27    Coach Jimmy Dugan in *A League of Their Own*: *".....there's no crying in baseball, THERE'S NO CRYING IN BASEBALL, no crying!"*

28    Some in outcasts had such a phobia about being "abnormal" that they began agitating  and creating chaos in an effort to do away with the concept altogether; note the following from *Gay is OK with the APA*, MEDICAL NEWS AND PERSPECTIVE, August 12, 1998:

*In 1973 Melvin Sebashin, MD, .......recalled "tumultuous demonstrations by gay activists objecting to the classification of homosexuality as an illness and by Viet Nam war protesters at the APA's annual meeting in San Francisco, Calif, in 1970, a year when he served as program director.* "*It was a guerilla theater," he said, "with lots of hard words," so disruptive, in fact, that the APA hired a security consultant to try to ensure more orderly demonstrations at future annual meetings. .......By 1973, however, there were exhibits at the meeting on being "gay, proud, and healthy."*

*(All this) was part of a broader movement to reexamine ideas about psycho-pathology in general, "to accept that all of us have some problem or another," and to redefine what is and is not normal. "The development of a rational (huh? dmh) approach to pathology," Sebashin said, "was salient and helpful to the gay group."* www.soulforce.org/article/642. The soulforce article may have been scrubbed. Try this other one: www.jama.jamanetwork.com/article.aspx?articleid=187846

(Translation:  The perpetual adolescents grabbed some Milk Duds and kicked and screamed until the decent people caved.)

29   FWIW, the formula for the curve is $y = \dfrac{e^{-x^2/2}}{\sqrt{2\pi}}$ . The shape of the curve is like the silhouette of a bell, hence the name "the bell curve":

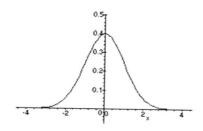

http://www.willamette.edu/~mjaneba/help/normalcurve.html.‗ Notice  the title of this section in the article: "Quick facts about the **_normal curve_**" (emphasis mine, dmh)

30   Thank you, Norman Bennett

31  It was worse than it should have been in the George W. Bush administration because he really did try to bring a new tone to Washington. In attempting this, he left a lot of Clinton appointees in power and even let Teddy Kennedy craft what could've been Bush's signature education reform.

32  Robert Bork, *Slouching Toward Gomorrah*

If you'd like to get a better understanding of the Chattering Class, go to Sojourners.com and do a quick study of the bios of the staff that lays claim to "Celebrating 40 years of faith in action". It's hard to find anyone associated with that organization who has done anything other than teach, write, "organize" or agitate. (I don't want to be misleading here, one of the staff does do something constructive – she's proud that she "plants food – vegetables, of course!") Classic Chattering Class. See appendix B.

33  It's just a coincidence, Birney. This has nothing to do with you.

34  Nikita Khrushchev's threat to the West, November 18, 1956: "We will bury you."

35  The first Gulf of Tonkin encounter.

36  The second "Axis of Evil" was famously (and accurately) identified by George W. Bush as being Iraq, Iran, and North Korea.

37  There's just this vague note in the Wikipedia account: "The United Kingdom, Russia, and the United states all agreed that Vietnam belonged to France."

38  The Geneva Accords (May 7, 1954) gave the French enough cover to save face and get back   to making wine and cheese.

You've heard the joke, right?  Goes like this:  "Hey buddy, wanna buy this French rifle?   It's never been fired and only been dropped once!"

39    I guess some Frisbee thrower could say Manifest Destiny was America's own despicable form of imperialism, but we have to be pragmatic about this: If the Americans and the Canadians hadn't settled the Great Plains, who would have fed the world?  If the world really is interconnected and "one", then the Indians were failing miserably in their stewardship of its resources.  And what about that "Survival of the Fittest" thing?  Is it valid or not?  Doesn't Darwinism tell us that if the Indians aren't "fit" they shouldn't survive?  (Hey, don't get upset with me, it's not my theory.)

40    Demilitarized Zone.  The dividing line between North and South Vietnam roughly along the 17th parallel.

41    One event where this opposition surfaced occurred on the Washington Mall, November 15, 1969.  The organizers of this demonstration had received praise from Pham Van Dong, Prime Minister of North Vietnam.  In a letter to the organizers, Dong said "... may your fall offensive succeed splendidly." This was the first time that the government of North Vietnam publicly acknowledged the American anti-war movement.  Dong's comments enraged American conservatives, including Vice President Spiro Agnew.  Agnew labeled the protesters "Communist dupes comprised of an effete corps of impudent snobs who characterize themselves as intellectuals."    http://www.bbc.co.uk/dna/h2g2/A715042

42    This is because they really do believe and try to practice the axiom "I never met a man I didn't like."   In other words, they do aim at decency.  In doing this they try to follow commandments like "Love thy neighbor as thyself," and "Follow after things which make for peace," and "Count the other better than yourself."

43    Barbarella was a ridiculous movie that used gratuitous sex to teach us...... nothing.  It starred Jane Fonda's nubile body.  Fonda later became known as "Hanoi Jane" because of her subversive support of  the Communists in North Vietnam.  (Note: this footnote is one place where I had to be true to my pledge of calling no one a fool.  For a while it said "....starred Jane Fonda's nubile body and empty cranium." But that was going too far.  So I repent, and now it's just a simple complement: "Jane Fonda's nubile body.")

44   As this sentence is being written, I'm in a Paris hotel, watching *"Bridge over the River Kwai."* It was released in 1957.

45   aka "draft dodgers"

46   In 1977, one day after his inauguration, President Jimmy Carter fulfilled a campaign promise by offering pardons to anyone who had evaded the draft and requested one. It antagonized critics on both sides, with the right complaining that those pardoned paid no penalty and the left complaining that requesting a pardon required the admission of a crime. Wikipedia, March 16, 2012

47   Walter Cronkite / CBS Evening News:"But it is increasingly clear to this reporter that the only rational way out then will be to negotiate, not as victors, but as an honorable people who lived up to their pledge to defend democracy, and did the best they could."

48   Abbie Hoffman, November 15, 1969.

49   November 9, 1989

50   March 9, 2005

51   On September 2, 1985, a Monday, Dan Rather surprised everyone at CBS by ending the news with, "Courage." The next day, Tuesday, he said it again. Executive Producer Tom Bettag asked him about it and told Rather to consult him if he wanted to change the daily sign-off. On Wednesday, Rather said it again. TV columnists began to call into CBS to inquire about this unusual closing. The senior staff of the broadcast met with him to try to talk him out of it. On Thursday, Rather didn't use "Courage." Instead, he said, "Coraje" (cor-a-heh). Inquirers jammed the CBS phone lines. One bureau chief said, "What the hell did he say?" to a New York producer. "I don't know, he either said the Spanish word for 'courage' or an Asian form of the martial arts." CBS's Bill Moyers had just done a story on the Mexican-American border and it must have given Rather Latin fever. On Friday, it was back to "courage."

In the meantime, other journalists began ridiculing Rather's fascination. Bryant Gumble of NBC's Today show poked fun with his own signoffs, "Valor," "Hot dogs," "Mazel tov." The next week, on Monday, Rather didn't say it at all. Some of the people in the Broadcast Center broke into applause.  *http://www.ratherbiased.com/courage.htm*

52   A poster in the window of a San Diego NBC affiliate has a picture of reporter Susan Taylor proclaiming: "Reporting isn't a job (sic) It's a calling". That statement could be true or false depending on which way it's meant. Are reporters "called" to report history, or change the future? Ask Susan Taylor.

53   Helter Skelter.   August 8, 1969.  This was when Charles Manson got a little impatient with how slow the PortHuronStatement was being implemented and decided to carve up a few regular citizens in order to help usher in the coming New Age.  Something like this horrific crime was probably inevitable, because Manson was mixing Scientology with LSD.

54   No originality here....besides the Bible, this quote is also attributed to Euripides (480-406BC), Maria Mitchall (1847), Georg Lichtenberg(1742-1799), Karl Marx, and Buddha Gautama.

55   I Thessalonians 5:21

56   This prejudicial mindset was formalized by Sonya Sotamayor in her lecture "A Latina Judge's Voice" given at UC Berkeley, 2001. It's also worthy to note she also argued that the "court of appeals is where policy is made." (2005)

57   5th Dimension, 1969

Also, note this comment from Wikipedia, 1/4/2012:  *"How do we know if the Age of Aquarius will be 'a utopia or an Orwellian nightmare'?"* Ray Grasse, *Signs of the Times*, 2002, Pgs228-231.

58    Tommy James & the Shondells, 1969. Note what James said about his song: "When I wrote Crystal Blue, it was taken from the book of Revelation: the imagery of the new Jerusalem."

59    Barack Hussein Obama, February 19, 2008

60    Ibid, 2007 Presidential campaign. Here's a humorous observation about that 57-state   comment:

"When every man, woman and child in America heard this statement ......., an amazing thing happened. For the first time in our young nation's history, each of us all had the exact same thought at the exact same time. The word-for-word, exact, same thought was *"(Darn), He is from Kenya."'* (http://www. cracked.com/funny-1872-silly-obama-qoutes/)

61    "Woodstock," sung by Crosby, Stills and Nash, 1969, written by Joni Mitchell

62    Genesis 11:1-9.  *"Let us make a name for ourselves....."*

63    The Mini Cooper is a small car fashionable with many Sierra Clubbers, whose morality is concerned primarily with saving Mother Earth.

64    Wikipedia: "Science is an enterprise that builds and organizes knowl-edge in the form of *testable* explanations and predictions about the natural world.  Please note the essential qualification "testable."

65    February 18, 2008, Michelle Obama *"For the first time in my adult lifetime I'm really proud of my country"*

66    "Humphrey" was the name given to the humpback whale, which made *two* attempts at   freshwater conversion, one in October, 1985, and again in 1990.

67  This dolphin event is fictionalized, but is based upon hundreds of dolphin beaching events that continue to occur around the globe.

68  Sagan's head was a featured hologram-like recording in the Smithsonian Air and Space Museum. If you want to get a feel for that performance go to the following link:

http://www.youtube.com/watch?v=HZmafy_v8g8&feature=youtube_gdata_player

69  Neil Diamond,1971

70  Super Tramp, 1979

71  Kansas, 1977

72  Kid's pizza parlor and party/game room popular since its inception in 1977.

73  *Polar Bears are Smarter than Al Gore*, Gregory Murphy.  This scientific study points out that populations are increasing in 18 of 20 polar bear groups, and that the decrease in two groups cannot reasonably be attributed to climate change, whether anthropogenic or not.  If you don't know what anthropogenic is, you have no business offering opinions on this subject.  Do you hear this, DarylHannah?

http://www.21stcenturysciencetech.com/Articles%202007/GW_polarbears.pdf

74  Hydroflurocarbons

75  Chlorofluorocarbons

76  Here's where this sexual ambiguity lunacy is headed:

"A British husband and wife who kept the sex of their child a secret for five years just spilled the beans: It's a boy. To avoid stereotyping, Beck Laxton and Kieran Cooper allowed their son, given the gender-neutral name of Sasha, to wear both "boy" and "girl" clothing. The Daily Mail said the parents called their child "the infant" to avoid using "he" or "she.""

http:family.lifegoesstrong.com/article/its-boy-update-one-gender-neutral-child.

77  "Although my ideas are in the earliest stages of development, they are, in my mind, worth investigating. One of my favorites is in the area of forest conservation which we heavily rely on for oxygen. I propose a limitation be put on how many squares of toilet paper can be used in any one sitting." Sheryl Crow, April 19, 2007

78  This is just to refresh your memory about the previous footnote about when Sarah Palin was asked about the "Bush Doctrine" by Charlie Gibson, and internet sites dealing with the subject were overwhelmed with changes. (Footnote #11)

79  Faith-based environmental groups hate the biblical word "subdue'. (Genesis 1:28)

80  We should treat animals "humanely," which means they're treated with respect for life because we're humans, not because they are animals. Obvious, isn't it?

81  Wikipedia, "Musica Universalis": The concept can be traced back to Jewish beliefs about an orderly cosmos hymning the praises of the (C)reator.

82  Dick Gephart, 1995

83  "It takes a Village to Raise a Child: And Other Lessons Children Teach Us" was a ghost written   book that Hillary Clinton claimed to author in March, 1996. Part of the title was taken from an ancient African proverb. For many the book came to symbolize forces working to destroy the traditional family. One is compelled to ask Hillary ""So, what did this ancient proverb do for ancient Africa?"

(Endnotes)

84 Friedrich Hayek (Quote in Wikipedia 2/13/2012)

85 Ben O'Neill (ibid.)

86 Janusz Korwin-Mikke (ibid.)

87 Barbarella weighs in again here. Hanoi Jane starred in the movie *They Shoot Horses Don't They?*

88 Money from Washington under the current administration is sometimes referred to as "Obama's stash."

89 It's instructive that the word "entitlement" didn't come into existence until 1942.

90 Merriam-Webster

91 From the movie *Legends of the Fall* -- I think.

92 http://www.factcheck.org/2008/04/blacks-and-the-democratic-party/

93 "Title 9 from Outer Space: How federal law is killing men's college sports." Walter Olson, *Reason Magazine*, February, 1998. This article also chronicles some of the hilarious liberal incompetence displayed while trying to enforce rules:

*Anyone at all can file a complaint that triggers an OCR (US Department t of Education's Office of Civil Rights) investigation, and such probes, as Pittsburgh Post-Gazette sports writer Lori Shontz observes, are not always known for their sophistication and subtlety. Staffers who swooped down on Johns Hopkins University, for instance, demanded to know why the women's basketballs were smaller than the men's', not realizing that "women's basketballs are smaller by design to accommodate smaller hands."*

94 It was a standing joke about Olympic gymnastics judging during the '70s, that the Eastern Bloc Communist judges gave Western performers ridiculously low scores.

95    The mythological name was revived in 1979 by James Lovelock in *Gaia: A New Look at Life on Earth*; his Gaia hypothesis was supported by Lynn Marquis. The hypothesis proposes that living organisms and inorganic material are part of a dynamic system that shapes the Earth's biosphere, and maintains the Earth as a fit environment for life. In some Gaia theory approaches the Earth itself is viewed as an organism with self-regulatory functions. (Wikipedia, 5//2/2012.)

96    1 Kings 3:23-28

97    TS Elliot

98    One example: The wildly unpopular Health Care Reform Act. I got to fly on a Saturday airline flight out of the Bahamas next to that liar Tom Harken (D-Iowa), who was in a state of near-panic about potentially not making it back to Washington for the vote.

99    Ecclesiastes 8:11

100    September 13, 2000.

101    San Franciscan Nights, Eric Burden and the Animals, 1967

102    Barack Hussein Obama, First presidential debate, August 17, 2008.

103    I won't give the reference here – I don't want to be responsible for ruining your day. But the videos of actual live beheadings can be found on the internet. Now, who does this? Who videotapes the beheading of an innocent bystander and then releases it to the public?

104    Trent Lott's "joke" about Robert Byrd (December 5, 2002)

105    Allen's "Macaca" remark at a campaign rally (August 11, 2006)

(Endnotes)

106    David Brooks was enamored with Barack Obama, apparently because of the crease in his pants.  September 1, 2009

107    "(Tom) Hayden also played a key role in the protests surrounding the 1968 Democratic National Convention in Chicago, Illinois.  Six months after the convention he was indicted on federal charges of conspiracy and incitement to riot as part of the "Chicago Eight," with other protesters including Abbie Hoffman and Jerry Rubin.  Wikipedia reference, 11/17/2010

108    It's just an educated guess, of course.  But the numbers are too impressive to ignore.

109    This part of the story is just rubbish on my part.  The Frisbee was design by Walter Frederick Morrison, who got a patent for it in 1958.  It was called the "Pluto Platter" at the time.

110    Students torched the Harvard ROTC on May 6, 1970 the one at Kent State on May 6, 1969, among many others.  Bill Ayers bombed the Pentagon on May 19, 1972.  This is what is meant when the Left says "Civil Disobedience."

111    Many church leaders are trying to "do grace" in this country while at the same time saying it's deserved, and calling it "social justice".  Can't be done without corrupting both divine principles.

112    A poster in the ATL airport propagandizes:

*People ask Santiago (Vanegas) "Why go to Antarctica?"  There are many reasons.  Most importantly, it will soon be a very different place.  As we speak, ice shelves the size of entire countries are breaking off the continent and melting into the ocean.  Antarctica is dying.*

113    "Man Up" was considered the #1 campaign catch phrase in 2010.  Sharon Angle, Robin Carnahan, and Kendrick Meek were among those employing it.  Sarah Palin cut right through the ambiguity and said Barack Obama lacked "cojones" when it came to border security.

114    http://www.ncdsv.org/images/ManUp_CampSelectsYoungLeadersStop VAW_3-7-10.pdf

115    Vice-President Dan Quayle was relentlessly ridiculed for misspelling the word "potato" at an elementary school spelling bee on June 15, 1992. The reference material here is Wikipedia. Something else interesting about this Wikipedia bio of Quayle. The summary of his vice-presidency is one paragraph dealing solely with ridicule about his verbal blunders. Contrast Quayle's Wikipedia treatment with Joe Biden's. Here's a summarizing quote: "Senior Obama advisor Valerie Jarrett said that Biden's loose talk '[is] part of what makes the vice president so endearing ... We wouldn't change him one bit'. Former Senate colleague Lindsey Graham said, 'If there were no gaffes, there'd be no Joe. He's someone you can't help but like'." (Wikipedia 08:28, 2/11/2012)

116    "Where in the World is Carmen Sandiego?" was a popular computer game first introduced in 1985.

117    From the plaque attached to the Nasa Lunar Lander. The full inscription reads: "Here men from the planet Earth first set foot upon the Moon. July, 1969. We came in peace for all Mankind."

118    "John Lennon was a closet Republican, who felt a little embarrassed by his former radicalism, at the time of his death - according to the tragic Beatles star's last personal assistant. Fred Seaman worked alongside the music legend from 1979 to Lennon's death at the end of 1980 and he reveals the star was a Ronald Reagan fan who enjoyed arguing with left-wing radicals who reminded him of his former self." http://www.torontosun.com/2011/06/28/lennon-was-a-closet-republican-assistant

119    Written by Dick Holler; sung by Dion, 1968.

120    Sanger is recognized as the founder of Planned Parenthood. In *A Plan for Peace* (1932), Sanger proposed forming a congressional department to:

"Apply a stern and rigid policy of sterilization and segregation to that grade of population whose progeny is already tainted or whose inheritance is such that objectionable traits may be transmitted to offspring."

(Endnotes)

121   Social Security, New Deal, Financial Reform

122   The Great Society

123   This figure comes from the now infamous National 10-year AGBM Study. (AGBM is an acronym for "A Guess By Me.")

124   <u>Freedom of Simplicity</u>, by Richard J. Foster (p106)

125   Florida Secretary of State, 1999

126   *Redemption Songs*, Bob Marley

127   *Rules for Radicals*

128   From the movie *Christmas Story.*

129   *"Don't Take Away Our Lipstick, Female Marines Protest,"* Marine Corps Times, September 10, 2001.(I kid you not, look it up, and pay close attention to the date.)

130   http://patdollard.com/2011/05/obama-hesitated-%E2%80%93-panetta-issued-order-to-kill-osama-bin-laden/

131   The Obama Coward Award, proposed on May 4, 2010

132   Newsweek Cover, May 31, 2012.

133   Genesis 19:1-25. Note also what the men of Sodom said to Lot when he refused to cooperate: v.9 "This man.....keeps acting like a judge...." Does that ring a bell? Ever hear someone accuse the decent people of being "judg-mental", or maybe "intolerant", when they take a stand for decency?

134   John McEnroe's first notable outburst. Wimbledon Tennis Tournament, 1981.

135   Dr. Katz was an animated series that ran on Comedy Central from 1995 to 1999.

136   Reference the movie "A Christmas Story"

137   http://blogs.muxlim.com/siecantik/can-makkah-mean-time-challenge-gmt

138   http://family.lifegoesstrong.com/article/its-boy-update-one-gender-neutral-child

139   http://www.infowars.com/climate-change-skepticism-a-sickness-that-must-be-treated-says-professor/

140   http://www.soulforce.org/about/why-religion/    Home page under "Why Religion?" (March 18, 2012)

141   The "someone" who pushed for this legislation in Illinois was Barack Hussein Obama.  For a first-hand account about what his legislation supports see the following video:

http://www.youtube.com/watch?v=NVNjrATbA20

142   http://www.infowars.com/ethicists-argue-killing-newborn-babies-should-be-allowed/

143   My apologies to Jim Ward, a non-wandering poet.